CROSSING BOUNDARIES
WITH
FRANK LLOYD WRIGHT

ALSO BY SIDNEY K. ROBINSON

Life Imitates Architecture: Taliesin and Alden Dow's Studio

Architecture of Alden Dow

The Prairie School in Iowa

The Continuous Present of Organic Architecture

Inquiry Into the Picturesque

CROSSING BOUNDARIES
WITH
FRANK LLOYD WRIGHT

HOW ORNAMENT LED TO ARCHITECTURE

CROSSING BOUNDARIES

WITH FRANK LLOYD WRIGHT

HOW ORNAMENT LED TO ARCHITECTURE

SIDNEY K. ROBINSON

 OA+D ARCHIVES PRESS   ARIZONA   2023

www.oadarchives.org

Library of Congress Cataloging-in-Publication Data

Names: Robinson, Sidney K., 1943– author.
Title: Crossing boundaries with Frank Lloyd Wright : how ornament led to
architecture / Sidney K. Robinson.
Description: Arizona : OA+D Archives Press, [2023] | Includes
bibliographical references and index.
Identifiers: LCCN 2023007583 | ISBN 9781938938689 (hardcover)
Subjects: LCSH: Wright, Frank Lloyd, 1867–1959—Criticism and
interpretation. | Decoration and ornament—Philosophy.
Classification: LCC NA737.W7 R63 2023 | DDC 720.92—dc23/eng/20230222
LC record available at https://lccn.loc.gov/2023007583

ISBN 978-1-938938-68-9 (hardcover)

Book design by Eric O'Malley

Printed and bound in the United States of America

To Alma and Richard
who gave me life and the freedom to live it

CONTENTS

ACKNOWLEDGMENTS
xi

FOREWORD
by David G. De Long
xiii

INTRODUCTION
1

ONE
*Examining Sullivan's Ornament
for Interpretation by Wright*
19

TWO
*Commentary on Ornament by
Wright and His Historical Context*
55

THREE
Crossing Boundaries in Wright's Writings
91

FOUR
Architectural Examples
133

CONCLUSION
185

NOTES
191

INDEX
203

ACKNOWLEDGMENTS

This effort spanned some years, and along the way many people have contributed through encouragement, counsel, and guidance. These include: John Waters, whose support, commitment, and invaluable contributions kept me going; Joan Iverson Nassauer, whose insightful commentary over the years clarified and focused my argument; Robert Bruegmann's and David De Long's welcome encouragement; Jim Erickson's steadfast belief in the effort; the contributions of Margo Stipe, Oskar Munoz, Kyle Dockery, and Ryan Hewson at the Frank Lloyd Wright Foundation; the skilled and generous contributions of Eric O'Malley; the photographers and delineators, especially Patrick Kinsfather and Thad Trejo; and Leslie Coburn, whose willingness to contribute her knowledge and discernment is the only reason this project was brought to successful completion, I owe more than I can say; and the many friends, including Greg Martin, David Kirby, and Lois Braverman, who remained supportive even as they wondered if all the repeated reports of activity would actually lead to a conclusion.

FOREWORD

David G. De Long

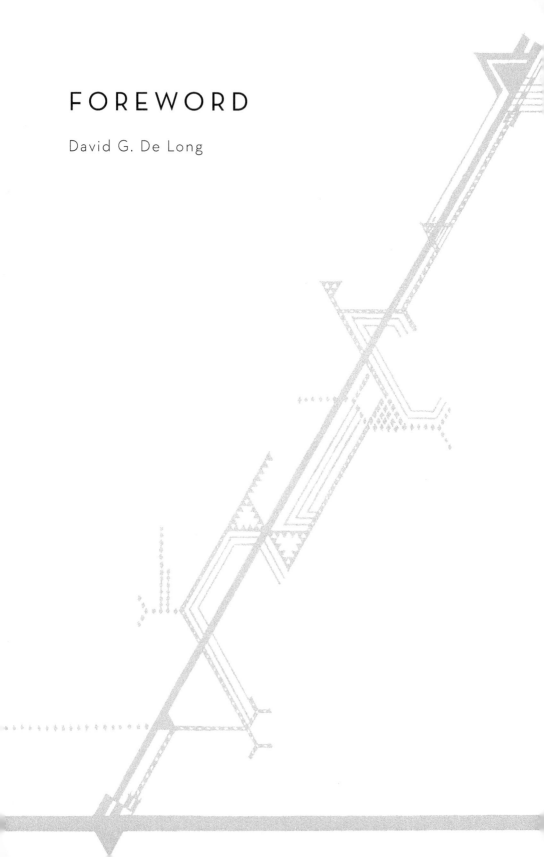

Frank Lloyd Wright challenged conventions and resisted fixed boundaries, freeing him to begin a new architecture. In his penetrating analysis of how he crossed those boundaries, and of the results that followed, Sidney Robinson provides new insights that advance our understanding of Wright's work and of his all-encompassing genius.

During a career that spanned from his first designs in the late 1890s until his death in 1959, Wright designed more than 1,000 buildings. He also designed countless related items, including furniture, tableware, fabric, graphics, and art glass. He was a voracious reader, not only of publications on architecture and the fine arts, but also poetry, fiction, history, biography, economics, philosophy, and drama, among others.

Understandably his work has been much studied, but his resistance to fixity, and to predictability, has complicated those efforts. Even defining what he meant by organic architecture—the term he used to explain his underlying philosophy of architecture—has proved difficult, as Edgar Kaufmann Jr.'s own definition reflects. Kaufmann, a former apprentice, important client, and adjunct professor at Columbia University, told me that he had spent several years refining this definition:

[Wright] saw human life as one of the processes of nature, not as some exceptional form of creation. Within nature people are active, adapting nature to suit their wants; they contribute feedback within the natural system. Similarly, he saw architecture as a natural process of human life, in turn nourishing its parent system. Thus to Wright architecture, humankind, and nature were joined in a grand dynamic continuity, and continuity within architecture indicated that people were aligning themselves—as he believed they should—with the natural forces of life.

Wright's concept of organic architecture imposed no fixed boundaries on building forms; structures were never meant to imitate nature, and designs did not employ those curvilinear shapes thought by many to embody forms of landscape. Instead, as seen at Fallingwater (the

Kaufmanns' country house, 1935–37), cantilevered rectangular terraces were crisply articulated, clearly a human intervention. Rather than imitating its setting, those terraces related to the projecting stone ledges below by clarifying their shapes, effecting the powerful unity between building and landscape that Wright sought. More broadly, the building joined its people to that landscape and through implication to the world beyond. Thus organic architecture was achieved.

Fallingwater also reflects Wright's unpredictability in its very siting. The family had bought the property in part because of its notable landscape—especially its dramatic falls. When Kaufmann's father and Wright first visited the site to discuss the commission in December 1934, the falls were a focus of their visit. But when Wright presented his designs, the family was astonished to see that instead of looking at the falls, as they expected, the house was to be placed over them. Kaufmann had encouraged his father to commission Wright and urged his father to proceed, later taking an active role in the realization of that extraordinary design. In later conversations, he related his parents' satisfaction with the completed house and said they felt more in touch with its landscape, and with nature, because of its design. Clearly Wright intended this very outcome.

While the ambiguities of Wright's organic architecture could be resistant to explanation, and conventions challenged by his siting of Fallingwater as well as by its daring structure, other boundaries that he crossed could be more be difficult to sense. Yet such crossings could be fundamental to Wright's approach in redirecting architecture, as Robinson explains. He also explains that however unexpected and unconventional Wright's work could be, underlying principles, by their very nature unencumbered by conventional boundaries, remained constant. Hence, just as Fallingwater's forms clarified the underlying structure of its natural setting, so ornament could make underlying structure of a deeper, more universal sort visible, establishing a yet more pervasive unity and thus adhering to a single principle.

Wright believed ornament essential to his architecture, and as he often stated, it was to be integral, never applied. Robinson focuses a major section of his analysis on the important place of ornament in Wright's work, arguing that in some cases his conceptions of ornamental form could even precede the buildings into which they were incorporated. Thus, while remaining true to principles, conventional boundaries separating ornament and architecture were crossed: ornament leads to architecture. This is no easy argument, but through analysis and specific examples, Robinson is persuasive, leading to a still deeper understanding of Wright's work and its meaning.

Wright often wrote about ornament, as Robinson recounts in his comprehensive review of Wright's publications, and he suggests clarifications often lacking in the writings themselves. Also prominent in Wright's writings are other terms, or categories, that he used in explaining his work and thought. Wright tended to attach broad meanings to these terms, and like his term *organic architecture*, their meanings are often obscure. In his text, Robinson discusses those of particular importance, furthering our understanding of Wright; in addition to *organic*, they include *machine*, *standardization*, *conventionalization*, *nature*, *history*, and *democracy*. In his use of these terms, Wright crossed boundaries by appropriating their customary meaning to suit his own approach, and explanations are welcome.

Examples of the buildings that Robinson cites illustrate more specifically how Wright crossed boundaries in his practice, and how crossing those boundaries could affect the forms of his buildings. Ultimately, it seems, form could be determined not only by conventional considerations, but also by the expression of some underlying pattern of idealized order, an order that could be first expressed through ornament. In his conclusion, Robinson reinforces his identification of this and related principles underlying Wright's work, offering an armature that later architects can follow so as to be in accord with Wright's architecture without mimicking it. A noble objective indeed.

INTRODUCTION

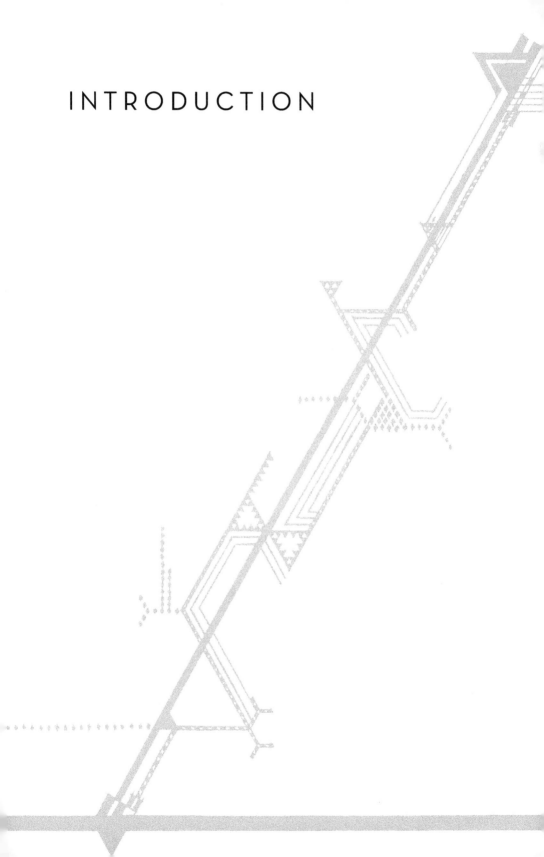

Frank Lloyd Wright's architecture is recognizable when we see his buildings. Their design is distinctive. The cantilevering roofs and angled walls, the response to the setting, the texture of projections and recesses all combine to characterize his architecture. Exploring how Wright constructed his formal compositions as the consequence of ideals at one scale and aesthetic choices at another is the focus of this narrative.

Wright himself makes connections between form and function, using his mentor Louis Sullivan's categories. However, more specific reasons for his choice of architectural forms are difficult to pin down. He chooses forms that activate the exterior perimeters and the complex envelopes of the interior spaces. Rather than reducing the relation of inside and out or room to room to a flat plane of separation, Wright constructs deep perimeters that project and recede across those borders. Both our eyes and our steps cross those boundaries.

The graphic design that opened Wright's *An Autobiography* can stand for a pattern that describes how he crossed borders in his architecture and in his commentaries on architecture. That graphic precedes the story of young Frank walking on a snow-covered hill on his Uncle John's farm in the vicinity of the home Wright would build some three decades later (fig. 1). As Wright relates the incident, his uncle proceeded up the hill in a straight line, the solid line in the graphic. The young boy, excited by the patterns of the dry weeds poking up through the snow, ran back and forth over his uncle's path collecting the weeds. On reaching the top of the hill, Uncle John directed the boy's attention back down the hill to the path of the adult's mature conviction. Frank saw something else. In his arms were the beautiful patterns of the weeds he had gathered in his crisscrossing footsteps. "Uncle John's meaning was plain—NEITHER TO THE RIGHT OR LEFT, STRAIGHT IS THE WAY. The boy looked at his treasure and then at Uncle John's pride, comprehending more than Uncle John meant he should. The boy was troubled. Uncle John had left out something that made all the difference."[1]

Figure 1. Graphic of zigzag path from Frank Lloyd Wright's *An Autobiography*.

This graphic design, which also appeared on the cover of an early edition of *An Autobiography* as further indication of its importance to Wright, is more than an ornamental abstraction of a childhood event. It stands for a whole way of thinking. The 30/60 triangular composition (what Wright called the "reflex angle" in the late 1920s conferring new significance on the draftsman's triangle) is anchored by the line of Uncle John's unwavering path. Wright's path of smaller, triangular patterns crosses back and forth, wrapping the strong armature with freedom

CROSSING BOUNDARIES WITH FRANK LLOYD WRIGHT

and delight. It does not seem inappropriate to correlate this geometric "foliation" wrapping around an armature to the design of Louis Sullivan's ornament whose geometric diagrams structured the efflorescence of the leaves. "The Sullivanian motif was efflorescent, exvolute, supported by tracery of geometric motive…" as Wright characterized it.[2] The armature and the efflorescence depend on each other.

The implications of this graphic design can be found in the forms of Wright's buildings, but it also diagrams how he considers categories like the *machine, standardization, nature,* and others. He approaches these issues alternatively as advocate and adversary as he crosses over the line separating those contrasting positions like the boy crossing his uncle's path in the snow. This crossing pattern expands the importance of these issues by continuously examining their contribution or challenge to his ideal of architecture.

The subject that contributes most significantly to the formal composition of Wright's architecture is how he interprets ornament alternately as detail and concept. Of course, Wright produced amazing ornamental designs, but the focus here is how he thought about the category of ornament as an abstract armature for his architecture. When Wright approaches ornament from the perspective of architecture and architecture from the perspective of ornament, he shows how ornament can be seen as an "integral" extrapolation from the forms of the building and, alternatively, that architecture can be seen as an extrapolation from the compositional structure of the concept of ornament. The categories of architecture and ornament traditionally face each other across the distinction of their relative significance; one is primary, the other is subordinate. Wright reversed that appraisal by empowering the composition of ornament to structure a whole building. As a result of that reversal, the concept of ornament became an abstract guide for architecture, not a repository of forms that can appear in the design of a building.

When Wright thinks and designs like the crossover graphic design, he finds unexpected implications in philosophical, spatial, functional, and structural patterns. The following narrative looks closely at the artifacts that follow this pattern. The examination is based on the practice of close reading. Focusing attention on the artifact, whether a building or a proposition is a commitment to valuing the building, design, and words as the starting point for interpretation, not some overarching evolution of art and culture. Others have presented exceptional correlations of cultural and historical contexts in which Wright worked: what he read, whom he admired, what he saw. The present story focuses elsewhere; Walt Whitman, for example, does not appear here.

The practice of starting commentaries and interpretations of artifacts with close observation was instilled in me in English classes in 1959–61 at Ann Arbor High School. We wrote a lot of poetry analyses using Laurence Perrine's *Sound and Sense* (1956) as the guide. The New Criticism basis for his pedagogy placed primary emphasis on looking at the artifact closely, taking the cues for understanding from the evidence in the work itself. That may be a necessary first step but is not a sufficient one. It cannot be the first and last stage in analysis and understanding as partisans of New Criticism sometimes claimed. When one had really examined the materials present in the work, steps would be taken to incrementally expand the references. However, the sequence from specific to more general resulted in a different valuation of the work than working the other way around, from general to specific. Wright may have recommended deductive reasoning, from principle to example, but in practice, induction operated in rapid alternation with deduction. Working from artifact to context and back, having started with the artifact, makes the encounter immediately engaging, but also guarantees that the foundation of meaning stays in the artifact.

Frank Lloyd Wright participated in what came to be called "Modern Architecture." One of the habits that set him apart from doctrinaire Modernism was his use of ornament. He was dismissed for "possessing the taste of a Victorian embroiderer" and by manifestos that rejected ornament as a symptom of 19th-century decadence.[3] Seeing past that revolutionary repudiation, Wright continued to produce significant examples in graphics, artifacts, and architectural embellishments. One has only to recall the rich ornamental programs in Midway Gardens (1914) and the Imperial Hotel in Tokyo (1923) to see that he clearly enjoyed producing a staggering number of drawings to direct the decorative efforts of masons, carpet manufacturers, leaded glass artisans, carpenters, and furniture-makers. Because European Modernism was being established contemporaneously with those two projects and then imported to the United States by the 1932 "Modern Architecture: International Exhibition" at the Rockefeller-funded Museum of Modern Art, the intense ornamentation of these buildings clearly set Wright apart from virulently ascetic proclamations coming out of Europe. Something more than embellishment kept Wright's interest.

Wright correlated ornament and architecture by seeing how they could both be derived from the same set of principles. Ornament grew out of the building's "grammar." That was "integral ornament," as Wright characterized it. But instead of the agency flowing in one direction, from building to ornament, Wright saw how the principles that produced ornament could appear in the design of the building itself. The leaded glass windows at the entrance of the Hardy House (1905) in Racine, Wisconsin (Figs. 1.2, 1.3), pose the question quite clearly: did an abstract pattern first direct the plan or the ornament? The plan's somewhat inconvenient arrangement of two levels of bedrooms separated in plan and on two floors sharing a half-level bath may be explained as human needs adjusting to an abstract pattern. Wright clearly sets up the reciprocity between form and function in a rather stunningly direct explanation of what comes first in the design process: "…until that [natural] pattern becomes a plastic, rhythmic fabric consistently adapted to human needs," his architectural goals cannot be achieved.[4] "Pattern . . . adapted to human needs" clearly puts form first, as a beginning, not an end.

Figure 2. Thomas Hardy House, Racine, Wisconsin.
Art glass window (reproduction). (Photo by Mark Hertzberg)

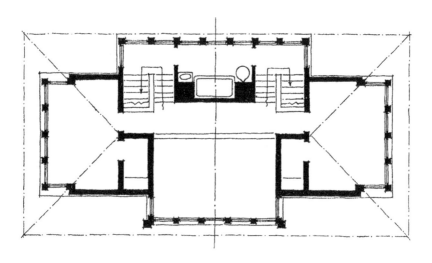

Figure 3. Plan of Thomas Hardy House.
(From *Wasmuth Portfolio of Buildings, Plans, and Designs,*
Horizon Press, New York, 1963 reprint)

Ornament was not "on" something, but "of" it. Wright saw this internal integration as characteristic of his mentor Louis Sullivan's ornament. In a powerful insight, he extrapolated Sullivan's principle of continuity within the ornament itself to "the building as a whole." Curiously, it was only late in life that he was able, or willing, to say what he saw in Sullivan's ornament: "I had seen [plasticity] in Lieber Meister's ornament....The ideal of plasticity was now to be developed and emphasized in the treatment of the building as a whole....This ideal, profound in its architectural implications, soon took another conscious stride forward in the form of a new aesthetic... called...continuity."[5]

Wright's own architectural ornament often sought to derive from the larger context of the building and its structure. But seeing how the coherence of ornament could be applied to a whole building, something Sullivan never did, Wright reversed the traditional practice of deriving secondary features from primary foundations. The word *structure* itself had more than one meaning for Wright; it was more than structures designed to resist gravity. When using it to describe the magic of his beloved Japanese wood-block prints, he referred to structure in this way: "Japanese art is a thoroughly structural art."[6] Structure was what composed parts into a coherent design just as structure in a building stabilized the parts of the building.

To pursue design from ornament to structure rather than from structure to ornament may seem a perverse reversal of hierarchical significance; the superficial should not direct the primary. Such reversals are how Wright thought about many things. His restatement of Sullivan's dictum "Form Follows Function" to read "Form and Function Are One" asserts that each could influence the other. Form can suggest function as much as function leads to form. Such an approach calls into question the proposition that there is a unique form for any function. Seeing function viewed from the perspective of form and form viewed from the perspective of function expands each of their potentials without intending to erase their characteristic differences.

Wright's predilection for crossing boundaries to define categories and forms going both ways is a major source of the depth and richness of his thought and architecture. That characteristic will be identified as "complex boundary" here. I cannot say that I have completely avoided the temptation to find complex boundaries most everywhere, much like the boy who is given a hammer and finds that the whole world just became a nail.

Wright himself proposed the surprising possibility that ornament could influence structure when he finally, in his eighth decade, sat down to write his testimony to his Lieber Meister, Louis Sullivan, in the 1949 publication *Genius and the Mobocracy*. He wrote:

> *Many years later as I lived, drew, and built I found in what I conceived and drew that the element I now call plasticity (the master had rendered it so completely in clay) carried in its own nature implications of unexplored structural continuity and could exemplify, simplify, and even prove the aesthetic validity of structural forms themselves....Plastic continuity is a product of these instructive spatial properties implicit in the work emanating from his own beautiful drawings.*[7]

To look at Sullivan's ornament and to interpret it as having structural implications is an unexpected reversal of conventional priorities. Wright's capacity to work across categorical boundaries may qualify him to be considered "modern," if one posits that word to be a call to erase or overturn conventional structures of thought and architecture. But more of that later. Wright's statement about what he learned from Sullivan, coming so late in his life, may be the result of Wright finally letting himself engage in reflection in his maturity. Or it may mean he no longer felt the need to avoid the appearance of influence or dependency. To admit learning from an example did not diminish Wright's sense of primacy since it took such a huge interpretive leap to get from Sullivan's ornament to Wright's own architecture. But this admission, if that is what it is, only appears two-thirds of the way into his testament to Sullivan. The announcement stands out if one can see past Wright's familiar bluster. In any case these statements are both a surprise and an illumination of what is characteristic of Frank Lloyd Wright's architectural goals.

The words Wright uses to explain how his insight led him from ornament to structure came from the two words Sullivan used to characterize his own ornament. "Plasticity" and "continuity" generated the amazing efflorescence in terra cotta, iron, plaster, and paint that embodied Sullivan's designs. How Wright expanded the potential that lay in their conjunction is further evidence of how his perception recognized differences even as it crossed over to see continuity. Continuity and plasticity, although descriptive of ornament, are equally present in the analysis of structure.

Plasticity is often used to point out a spatial quality of recess and projection in the third dimension. When applied to sculpture, *plastic* is contrasted with *planar*. Plasticity describes an interaction of artifact and environment that is complex, not reducible to a singular, flat relation. Wright explored the complex boundary which differentiates between the internal conditions within an artifact and the external conditions of its setting. The description and interpretation of such a relationship requires a continuous dialog rather than a clear distinction. Wright saw this quality in the malleable materials of clay, metal, and plaster that Sullivan used in his ornament. It also describes the masterful way Sullivan drew his ornament as highlights and shadows. Sullivan was most fortunate that there were craftsmen who could "read" that representation of projection and recess and manifest it in metal and clay.

The word *continuity* emphasizes the connection between elements, large or small, in a composition. It directs attention to what is shared or in common. "Through-composition" in music is an example of continuity.

Beethoven's Fifth Symphony is a premiere example in Western classical music: a four-note motif underlies the whole symphony. Wright explicitly saw this connection: "What I am here calling integral-ornament is founded upon the same organic simplicities as Beethoven's Fifth Symphony,... built on...four repeated tones, simple rhythms..."[8] Continuity is not contiguity; it is not adjacency, let alone propinquity. For Wright, the words *plasticity* and *continuity* have a degree of overlap, but their differences are significant as one considers one and then the other. When he uses one as a modification of the other: "plastic continuity," their relationship is further complicated. Twenty years before he wrote *Genius and the Mobocracy*, Wright presented the source for the concepts of plasticity and continuity to be the lessons he learned from Sullivan. In the "Two Lectures on Architecture" written in October 1930 for the Art Institute of Chicago six months after delivering the Kahn Lectures at Princeton, he explicitly makes the connection: "The word *plastic* was a word Louis Sullivan himself was fond of using for this scheme of ornamentation, as distinguished from all other or any applied ornament."[9] But Wright extends the concept: "not merely as form following function, why not a larger application to this element of plasticity considered as *continuity* with the building itself....Instead of two things, one thing...plasticity, now *continuity*."[10] In a previous Princeton lecture, he had said: "'Plasticity' is of utmost importance."[11] He goes on to apply it to the "nature of materials," and he repeats the connection he had made between ornament and structure in his lecture "Art and Craft of the Machine" in 1901, when, as a 34-year-old, he was already focusing on a new form of connection, or continuity, that will appear "flowing or growing" to replace "cut and joined pieces." The structural implication he came to see in Sullivan's ornament was yet to be identified in 1901, but the habit of thought to do so was already in place.

A singular demonstration of Wright's search to link ornament and structure is found in the 1905–1907 Unity Temple in Oak Park, Illinois. The evolution of the design of the ornament inside Unity Temple can be traced because there are drawings that show the three major stages of the interior from fall 1905 to 1907. In brief, the sequence goes from a more conventional use of ornament that emphasizes the post-and-beam structure to a radical dissociation of structure and ornament, or, more accurately, to a whole new synthesis. Wright comes to use ornament to anticipate a yet-to-be-realized architecture. The experimentation he pursued in the ornament was used not just for decoration, but as diagrams of architectural possibilities.

Wright's initial design of the interior of Unity Temple had almost no ornament. Its primary focus emphasizes the conventional post-and-beam structure of the piers and balconies (fig. 4). The second stage adds ornament to the top of the four corner piers, clearly an adaptation of the recently finished Larkin Building in Buffalo, and wood strips to the fronts and undersides of the balconies (fig. 5). The applied wooden stripping introduces the means that will be used to completely revise the relation of ornament and structure when the interior is completed. Beginning as outlines of framed panels, the stripping we see today wraps structural elements with lines that clearly do not reinforce their familiar distinct functions (fig. 6). The continuous surface of the concrete structure is emphasized rather than the separation of the conventional structural elements. The most striking instance of this transformation is the ceiling pattern that overruns the top structural element of the piers, the abacus. The folding of the surfaces, as indicated by the wood strips, suggests a wholly new way to think of structure. Folded planes (he refers to them as "screens") replace solid blocks as the structure.

The development of this new conception of structure will be taken up subsequently. What is evident in Unity Temple is how Wright explores architectural and structural possibilities through ornament. It stands to reason that ornament's freedom from functional requirements makes it a perfect site for abstract speculation. Wright saw beyond conventional categories of ornament and structure to the overlapping patterns that

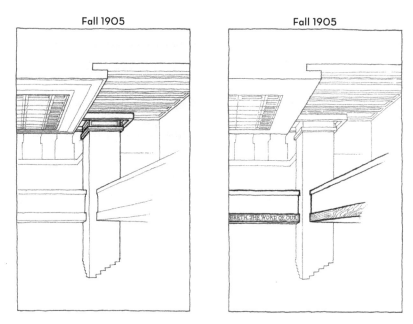

Fall 1905   Fall 1905

Figure 4. Unity Temple, Oak Park, Illinois. Initial interior design of conventional structural members. (Drawings by Patrick Kinsfather)

included both. That overlap meant he could cross over the conventionally defined boundaries that separate categories from the position of advocate and that of critic and back.

His early exposure to the Kindergarten Gifts of Friedrich Froebel is rightly recognized as a source for his placement of geometry at the center of the way he structures his designs. The investigative freedom he mentions as he plays with the strips of colored paper, the grid patterns as well as the famous blocks stayed with him even as his capacity grew to interpret them way beyond childish play. "…the straight line, square, triangle, and circle I had learned to play with in Kindergarten were set to work in this developing sense of abstraction,…"[12] Finding ways to stack the blocks to look like some of his buildings is basically an affront to his interpretive powers. What he learned handling the "gifts" was much more foundational than mere visual parallels. The delight in working with the materials certainly laid the basis for further creation.

CROSSING BOUNDARIES WITH FRANK LLOYD WRIGHT

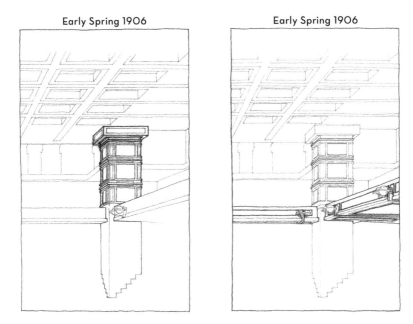

Early Spring 1906   Early Spring 1906

Figure 5. Unity Temple. Interior ornament emphasizing conventional architectural elements. (Drawings by Patrick Kinsfather)

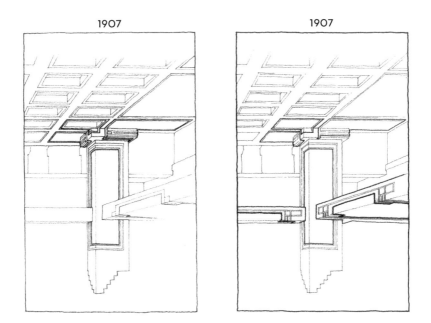

1907   1907

Figure 6. Unity Temple. Final interior folding ornament around architectural elements. (Drawings by Patrick Kinsfather)

Wright explored such crossings-over early in the "Art and Craft of the Machine" (1901). In this early statement, fourteen years after arriving in Chicago as an aspiring twenty-year-old, he defines the old art of building "fashioned when the handicraft…imposed layer upon layer in the old structural sense…wherein this form and that form as structural parts were laboriously joined in such a way as to beautifully emphasize the manner of joining."[13] The new art of building would not celebrate joints but express continuity and plasticity.

In the Princeton Lectures three decades later, those important reflective and stock-taking lectures delivered when he was in his sixties, Wright described his architectural goals in terms of plasticity and continuity. "Some years later I took continuity as a practical working principle of construction into the actual method of constructing the building. But to eliminate the post and beam, as such, I could get no help from the engineer. By habit, engineers reduced everything in the field of calculation to the post and girder before they could calculate anything and tell you where and just how much. Walls that were part of floors and ceilings, all merging together and reacting upon each other the engineer had never met and the engineer has not yet enough scientific formulae to calculate for such continuity."[14] He goes on to describe the stiffened slabs becoming cantilevers, welds replacing rivets all to provide "this new element of plasticity," but this is couched in terms of economy in construction. In passing he mentions the "soundness of the aesthetic idea," but does not elaborate. The synthesis of form, structure, and function was just around the corner, however. The coordination of those aspects of a building meant they each contributed to an integral conclusion. Wright often used the word *integral* to characterize his own ornament; ornament was not "on" something, it grew out of its setting. It was not a separate, separable thing, but another expression of the spirit sustaining the whole composition that flowed from the building and reciprocally flowed from the ornament back into the building. Integer has a singular aspect; one thing, not many. But immediately we must recognize that the proposition of unifying the parts in favor of the whole does mean the total merging of parts so as to give up all their individuality. This clearly has both formal and social implications.

Walking into the Phoenix Art Museum in 1990 to see a major exhibition of Wright's drawings led me to a gallery of full-scale drawings for the ornamentation of the Imperial Hotel in Tokyo. I was overwhelmed not only by the number of drawings, but by the evidence of how important and satisfying all this work must have been for Wright. One would not exert all that energy and time if one would rather be thinking about something else. To me these sheets of geometric efflorescence were proof of how much ornament meant to Wright. Tacking down the paper, assembling the T-square, triangles, and the compass had to quicken Wright's imagination. It is evident that making patterns pleased the eye, but also engaged the mind.

The connection between mind and eye is what can be discovered in the introductory graphic in the *Autobiography* mentioned earlier. It also serves to connect Wright to the world of contemporary architecture. That graphic likely also had a pointed target: contradicting his French nemesis Le Corbusier. Corbusier had recently published his book *Urbanism*, translated as *The City of Tomorrow and Its Planning*, in 1929. Wright had written a review in 1928 of Corbusier's previous book *Towards a New Architecture* published in English in 1927. Wright was paying attention, as he always did, to what other significant architects were doing. Corbusier opens his *City of Tomorrow* with a parable: "The Pack-Donkey's Way and Man's Way." "Man walks in a straight line because he has a goal....The pack-donkey...zigzags...in a scatter-brained and distracted fashion." It is just possible that Wright wanted to contradict his French colleague and chose to open his own story by telling of the power and reward of the zigzag.[15]

Beyond that challenge, the graphic introducing *An Autobiography* also shows how the pattern of the straight line and the crisscrossing reinforce each other. It is not one supplanting the other. Wright understood how the two patterns worked together throughout his whole career. The straight line also marks a boundary between two zones. Wright saw that such a stark separation did not describe either human or nature's action. He could have gathered the weeds in a line parallel to Uncle John's path after all. This graphic also diagrams one of Wright's metaphors of weaving as the thread of the weft crossed back and forth over the warp. The complex boundary, not its erasure, made interpretations possible both functionally, and intellectually.

The graphic that begins and recurs throughout this narrative is a diagram I have chosen to suggest how Wright crossed boundaries to gain reciprocal perspectives in his buildings and his writings. I am directing attention away from looking for its pattern in his architecture by proposing that its geometry, although undeniably attractive as a graphic pattern, is also an abstraction of Wright's way of working. The simultaneity of geometry as visible form and as underlying structure is the heart of his designs. Wright found that structure when he saw Louis Sullivan creating the abstract continuity and plasticity of his ornament. Wright's astonishing accomplishment was to interpret that abstraction beyond the visible pattern to compose the structure of a whole building. This interpretation is how ornament led to architecture.

As Wright tries to describe how he crossed boundaries, his prose is often hard to read because the expectation of simple descriptions linking principle to form is frustrated by a sequence of changing perspectives that can look like contradictions. The conventional expectation that one can find a form that illustrates a statement or that a parallel chronology of Wright's propositions and his buildings can be established is set aside here.

It is clear by this brief introduction that Frank Lloyd Wright's love of patterns, his persistent pursuit of them in the world around him, i.e., nature, and his ability to see/find them at many scales—ornament and architecture—appears in much of his work. When he was finding and making ornament, intellectual activity was often tracking the visual. Manipulating form provided Wright with a discipline that paralleled his consideration of function, structure, human relations, and even philosophy. Building an architecture on the principles of ornament is the primary way Wright demonstrated his cross-over approach to design and thought. The relation of ornament to architecture is the foundation of the complex boundary that would underlie buildings and words throughout Frank Lloyd Wright's career.

From here, I will trace the way Sullivan's ornament could be read as lessons in complex boundaries, as demonstrations of continuity and plasticity and how spatial concepts of plane and perspective stimulate consideration of the relation of two and three dimensions. Further exploration of the role that ornament was taking early in Wright's career records how ornament was being examined at the turn of the 20th century. The presence of complex boundaries in the way Wright thinks about things, particularly architecture is evident in his writings. The very aspect that makes Wright's writing sometimes confusing is owing to this boundary-jumping as he proposes, qualifies, and restates his approach to his art. In conclusion, there will be a suggestive set of examples of how Wright's architecture is structured by complex boundaries.

CHAPTER ONE

EXAMINING SULLIVAN'S ORNAMENT FOR INTERPRETATION BY WRIGHT

The pattern being examined here, Frank Lloyd Wright crossing boundaries, is most significantly found in the way he interpreted ornament reciprocally as detail and as model for architecture itself. He crossed over the conventional definition that he saw his mentor Louis Sullivan illustrating with his amazing foliated ornament. Wright saw beyond Sullivan's clay, metal, and wood examples by expanding the meaning of the terms Sullivan used to describe his ornament: *plasticity* and *continuity*, to animate the whole building.

The term *continuity* describes how the parts of the composition follow an order, a rule of combination that ensures that their individual contribution is to the whole ornament or building. Wright establishes this rule through geometry that guides both the part and whole. Plasticity, on the other hand, describes how the parts step forward in their individual role. If continuity were dominant, the parts would be overcome by the whole. Plasticity describes how the parts can rise up into the third dimension, expressing their identity. An example of how the two worlds of ornament and architecture can have this reciprocal relation may be found by setting a study for a leaded glass window in Midway Gardens next to an Oak Park Playhouse of 1926 (fig. 1.1). The 30/60 degree angles in the graphic design are lifted off the surface of the paper to bend and fold in the roofs of the Playhouse. I am hesitant to use this time-honored practice of finding things that look alike, but here it may serve to illustrate the general pattern of crossing over from one genre to another. Although the roofs of the Playhouse expand beyond the predominantly orthogonal patterns of the Prairie School years, the plan of the Playhouse remains in the orthogonal/octagonal world. The 30/60 "reflex angle" as Wright comes to refer to it, appears in plan only years after he has been using it in elevation and section. The windows in the Prairie houses have angles, of course, but they are invariably contained within the rectilinear discipline of the architectural context, just as the minimally sloped hipped roofs of the Prairie houses are framed by the orthogonal plans they shelter. The angles of the Playhouse roof raise the

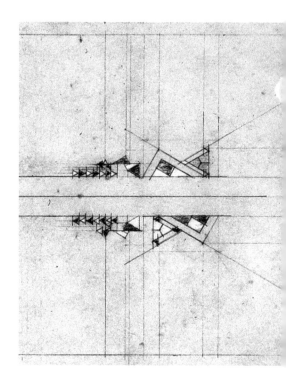

Figure 1.1. Midway Gardens Glass Design (right) and Oak Park Playground Association Playhouse Perspective (opposite page). Frank Lloyd Wright Foundation Archives: architectural drawings, ca. 1885–1959. The Frank Lloyd Wright Foundation Archives (The Museum of Modern Art | Avery Architectural & Fine Arts Library, Columbia University, New York) and Taliesin West archive.

angles of the Midway Gardens window into the third dimension with the geometry of a flattened hexagon that is not quite 30/60. Wright's subsequent incorporation of the 30/60 "reflex angle" into plan as well as elevation is further evidence of how continuity between ornament and architecture, and plasticity as the three-dimensional means to raise a graphic pattern into architecture, generate Wright's reciprocal perspectives of ornament and architecture.

It is very clear that Frank Lloyd Wright's use of ornament as detail diverged significantly from Louis Sullivan's as Wright set aside "Lieber Meister's" botanical efflorescence to explore geometrical elaboration. Immediately after contact with Sullivan, Wright's ornament is distinctive, but identifiable as having absorbed patterns learned at Sullivan's side in the Auditorium Building. He went on to simplify Sullivan's two-step

process that began with a geometric trellis then wreathed with foliation by making the geometry the content of the ornament: one step instead of two. To set the context of Sullivan's ornament that led to Frank Lloyd Wright's radical interpretation, the ornamental examples from the Banqueting Hall in the Auditorium Building (1890), will be examined with references to Sullivan's 1924 publication *A System of Architectural Ornament*.[16] These early examples are chosen because there are sixteen different ornamental patterns and because they were being produced when Wright entered Sullivan's studio. The later analysis by Sullivan is a summation of the origin, evolution, and development of his approach to ornament. Of course, Wright did not see that analysis when he was at Sullivan's side, but it systemizes the potential Wright found inherent in Sullivan's ornament.

Figure 1.2. Detail of Pilaster 16 and Pilaster 1, with lunette windows above, in the Banqueting Hall, Auditorium Building, Chicago. (© 2000 Nathan Kirkman)

The Banqueting Hall was added to the program of the Auditorium Building after construction had begun. It was in effect a room, 36 x 86 feet, supported by two trusses spanning above the auditorium proper. The walls of the long room were divided by eight pilasters separated by leaded glass lunettes above (fig. 1.2). Each pilaster capital was ornamented with a different composition. Rather than giving material form to Sullivan's drawings through the repeatable materials of clay or plaster, these different pilasters were individually carved from red birch. Tim Samuelson, the eminent cultural historian of Chicago, reports that the wood carvers (R. W. Bates and Company, cited by David Van Zanten) managed to approach the fluidity of plaster ornamentation that Sullivan was achieving elsewhere in the Auditorium Building by having the wood carvers refer to plaster models.[17] These three-dimensional examples enhance the compositional goal present in Sullivan's drawings. The unique carvings enabled Sullivan to display a whole range of ornamental patterns of unequalled richness and variety. The carving emerges from the

Figure 1.3. Banqueting Hall Pilaster 1.
(© 2000 Nathan Kirkman)

flat surface of the pilaster, turns horizontal to the underside of the large, projecting impost block, and turns vertical to spread over the face of the block. Although we will proceed along the walls, it cannot be said that Sullivan expected his ornamental display to be seen by a peregrination of contrast and revelation. However, two drawings of the pilasters are numbered so that a sequence Sullivan used can be followed.

PILASTER 1

Basing the sequence suggested by Sullivan's two numbered drawings, 15 and 16, we can begin number 1 at the north pilaster by the entrance (fig. 1.3). Eight mandorlas resulting from seven intersecting circles hide under a symmetrical explosion of seven leaves rooted on the underside of the block. The distinctive form of these and other leaves clearly have precedents in Gothic foliation. They are not soft, rounded leaves, but sharp, spikey ones. The inherent point and line of

Figure 1.4. Banqueting Hall Pilaster 2.
(© 2000 Nathan Kirkman)

these leaf forms helps the organic to crossover to the inorganic geometry (or the other way around!). This north pilaster is a dense combination of geometry underlying the plant forms that follow its lead. Layers of compositional structure completely occupy the ornament. There is no "surface" from which they spring. That is why the necking ornament is so important since it clearly emerges from the plain surface of the pilaster.

PILASTER 2

The compound pilaster at the corner north of the entrance wall is similarly dense in the overlapping of geometrical and foliate forms (fig. 1.4). The major impost face is composed of seven vertically elongated, ogee-arch hexagons framing a second layer of foliate forms that grow over the hexagon frames. Behind these leaves is a flat band the width of the long vertical edges of the hexagons. In contrast, the necking on the

Figure 1.5. Banqueting Hall Pilaster 3.
(© 2000 Nathan Kirkman)

pilaster face is a composition of leftward-facing, mandorla-like foliation that wrap around the corner. Further complexity fills the spaces between the ogee-arch frames with seven different foliate patterns.

PILASTER 3

The first pilaster to the north of the entrance wall displays a firm geometric control of four horizontally elongated octagons (fig. 1.5). The strict geometry continues to the squares at top and bottom between the octagons and the framing bands at the edges of the face. Inside the octagons are foliate patterns tightly controlled and centered on smooth ovals in the two center panels and a single swirl of leaf forms at the ends. The underside of the impost block is similarly lined with octagons. The fold from this horizontal plane to the pilaster from is accomplished with a recessive octagon filled with flattened leaf forms.

Figure 1.6. Banqueting Hall Pilaster 4.
(© 2000 Nathan Kirkman)

PILASTER 4

The geometric pattern of four circles in the next pilaster block lies beneath swirling bands of "stems" that culminate in sprays of leaf forms that could be terrestrial or aquatic (fig. 1.6). A background plane on which this foliate activity is played is more evident in this example and others. The pattern is "on" something here. The necking is similarly a four-part composition of vertical stems and leaves.

PILASTER 5

Seven stem/leaf motifs springing from left to right cover the face of the next pilaster impost block (fig. 1.7). A finely carved series of interlaced circles bands the bottom of the face. This closely structured band is a considerable contrast with the powerful foliate growth emerging from the face of the smooth pilaster. The energy of this symmetrical growth spreading up and under the block is then terminated by the band

Figure 1.7. Banqueting Hall Pilaster 5.
(© 2000 Nathan Kirkman)

of small circles at the edge of the face and by the beaded band from which the seven leaf-forms grow.

PILASTER 6

The density of geometry and foliage is a striking contrast to the figural compositions of the previous examples (fig. 1.8). This impost block is more texture than figure and the contrast with the smoothly articulated nine ovals could not be more arresting. The dense texture can be analyzed as interlocking squares and diagonal squares intertwined with symmetrical curving twists looking at once arabesque and Jacobean. The top and bottom of the impost face sprouts repeated horizontal leaf forms that turn underneath. The necking grows out of the smooth face and turns its diagonal geometry into the foliage of the underside. This example is so distinctive in part as a result of the scale of the motifs and their density. The combination of foliate forms and geometry is another

Figure 1.8. Banqueting Hall Pilaster 6.
(© 2000 Nathan Kirkman)

Figure 1.9. Banqueting Hall Pilaster 7.
(© 2000 Nathan Kirkman)

Figure 1.10. Banqueting Hall Pilaster 8.
(© 2000 Nathan Kirkman)

step in exploring that interaction, but rather than merging them as in the face of the block, the relation to the necking is abrupt.

PILASTER 7

The dominant motif of the next pilaster and impost block is geometry; there is almost no foliage and what is present is completely contained by the extended octagons and the half-circles that overlap them (fig. 1.9). The centers of the polygons are where the base, stem-like stalks sprout. The necking again emerges from the pilaster face and immediately is lost in the patterns of the face turned underneath.

PILASTER 8

The last pilaster on the north wall is another contrasting composition of geometric block and foliate necking (fig. 1.10). The four crisscrossing squares delineated by pairs of flat bands are laid on a small grid background behind the center Xs and frame four foliated bursts. The swirls of leaves at the necking revolve up and down and, like the neighboring example, are completely displaced by the geometry of the faces turned to the underside.

PILASTER 9

Beginning with the pilaster on the east wall opposite the entrance we see a band at the necking under the impost block, of twelve mandorla, pointed ovals that are complete at the underside of the block whose patterns shift abruptly to foliation (fig. 1.11). At the change in plane a completely different, non-geometrical, intricate foliation is organized as circular elements on the underside and the face of the impost block. There is only the slightest overlap of the upper foliation down onto the pilaster face. The structural distinction between a pilaster and an impost block is preserved by the different ornamental patterns.

The leaf-like forms, in a spiral pattern, are not repeated exactly. The four main spiral variations are in a kind of progression from left to right with decreasing geometrical focus underlying the foliation. The stems of the leaf spirals spiral out to link the first three but seem attenuated when arriving at the last one. The general outline of the four spirals is repeated, but the geometry governing composition is strikingly loose.

Sullivan's *A System of Architectural Ornament*, Plate 6: "Manipulation of Variants on a Given Spiral Theme," presents a comparable exposition of spiral leaf-forms in Pilaster 9, but the examples Sullivan drew are singular, not in series. As a result, these drawn examples stand alone as exercises without physical context. When the impost block frames a horizontal rectangle, the isolation of the analytical example must be adapted. Is the "inconsistency" of the pattern of spirals in the pilaster face a formal choice, and if so, what might be the goal? I cannot say. Maybe it was the carver's fault or choice. There are series examples in the *System*, but the geometric consistency is always clear enough to be recoverable by observation.

Figure 1.11. Banqueting Hall Pilaster 9.
(© 2000 Nathan Kirkman)

Figure 1.12. Banqueting Hall Pilaster 10.
(© 2000 Nathan Kirkman)

Figure 1.13. Banqueting Hall Pilaster 11.
(© 2000 Nathan Kirkman)

PILASTER 10

The next pilaster moving south along the east wall seems to continue the exploration of looser compositions (fig. 1.12). The change in ornamental patterns between the orthogonally related planes is similarly distinct as in the previous example, although at the corners of the pilaster, stemmed foliation springs and spreads out on the underside of the block. The impost block face is primarily symmetrical in its ornamentation with two mirror spirals (an echo of Ionic?) linked together by straps that loop and cross at the center of the face. What is striking, however, is the asymmetrical loop at the bottom of the face. This small, but strategic disruption of static symmetry may have its role described in *A System of Architectural Ornament* by Plate 10, "Fluent Parallelism: (Non-Euclidian)," or in Plate 15, "Values of the Multiple Leaf: Differential Energy." Both of these plates celebrate non-symmetrical forms so different from the majority of the other plates. In the pilaster, fan-shaped leaf patterns frame

CROSSING BOUNDARIES WITH FRANK LLOYD WRIGHT

the edges of the block and cover its underside. This "contest" between geometry and botany is one of the things that makes these exercises so fascinating. Sullivan makes this interaction a clear concern when he set up the Inorganic (Plate 1) and Organic (Plate 2) as the initiating sources for his ornament in his summary in *A System of Architectural Ornament*. I think it is significant that inorganic comes first, reflecting the sequence Sullivan used when setting out to draw the ornament: T-square and triangle first, soft pencil leaves subsequently. In Plate 7 he explains how this inorganic starting point leads to the "transition…from inorganic toward organic," clearly pointing out what comes first. Wright's insight going beyond Sullivan was that he could cross over and back seeing inorganic and organic each in terms of the other. Wright traversed this boundary crossing as he described the geometric pattern that underlay the Japanese print artist's rendering of natural forms. In this way he found the inorganic in the organic. Of course Wright expected to find inorganic patterns when he went to Japanese prints and plants; he found the geometry he was looking for. In the *System of Architectural Ornament*, Sullivan reversed that sequence by showing how organic patterns of growth could animate geometry. The possibility that Wright developed his art crossing over from both directions should be considered as a key to Wright's work.

PILASTER 11

Pilaster 11 may be seen as an even more direct quotation of the Ionic order capital (fig. 1.13). The spirals at the edges of the impost face are distinct, although compressed by the powerful context of a base molding that rises up to clearly hold the whole composition separate from the ornament of the pilaster below. This lower pattern is symmetrical with two arched forms filled with organic swirls. The pattern bends to the horizontal face of the impost block gently eliding the difference between pilaster and block. The face of the block framed by a strong, plain base barely overlapped by vegetal forms is similarly symmetrical with two

Figure 1.14. Banqueting Hall Pilaster 12.
(© 2000 Nathan Kirkman)

serrated discs at the center, but not quite equally symmetrical since the right-hand one overlaps the left. Between the corner spirals and these discs, a flowing continuation of the spiral is heavily foliated. The role of symmetry in Sullivan's ornament lies at the heart of the combination of geometry and plant forms. He links the two sources through the "seed germ," that he illustrates as a symmetrical opening of a seed along an axis. The axis is what guides geometrical as well as botanical development. Sullivan identifies the form that departs from the seed germ model as the expansion of axes. "There is always supposed to be a main axis:— however much it may be overgrown or overwhelmed by the vitality of its sub-axes."[18] The combination of static geometry, the inorganic, and the vitality of the organic creates the energy of formal exploration seen in these Banqueting Hall pilasters.

Figure 1.15. Banqueting Hall Pilaster 13.
(© 2000 Nathan Kirkman)

PILASTER 12

The next pilaster ornament furthers the expressive complexity of Sullivan's ornament (fig. 1.14). Geometry reigns supreme. Tightly contained geometric frames control the foliage. The face of the impost block has spiral leaves at the edges completely contained by the banding that continues to the center of the block to form a rectangle with seven tightly serialized vertical plant motifs. Bands at the top and bottom of the block are repeated forms; arrow shaped above and a kind of bead-and-reel below. In the face of the theory of inorganic and organic, the whisper of historical patterns is surprising. Where the previous banding at the top of the smooth pilaster was distinctly separate from the impost block's underside, in this example the hexagons merging into mandorlas appear incrementally out of the plane. It is as if the geometric pattern was already present in the organic material and was liberated by the "excavation" of

Figure 1.16. Banqueting Hall Pilaster 14.
(© 2000 Nathan Kirkman)

Figure 1.17. Banqueting Hall Pilaster 15.
(© 2000 Nathan Kirkman)

the carver. Further merging is evident at the transition from the vertical to the horizontal of the underside of the impost block. The angled forms bend and join a surface filled with organic patterns. The separation of "column" and "capital," if one can so characterize these elements, is giving way to a joining of elements.

PILASTER 13

The geometric control of the previous example is completely overgrown in the next pilaster (fig. 1.15). This example is all foliation, albeit in a strictly symmetrical pattern; the "seed form," after all, is symmetrical. The center of the necking on the face of the pilaster, and both the underside and face of the impost block, is the stem or axis for the exuberant leaf forms in high relief. At this central axis, the foliation of the necking grows over the edge to join the face ornament. This is the first example that clearly demonstrates the ideal that the ornament is not "on" a surface. The leaves are what would ordinarily be called the "surface"; that is to say, there is no evidence of a plane underlying or supporting the foliation. That is particularly striking at the necking, which has an explicit boundary separating the ornament from the plane of the pilaster. But it too is not seen to be "on" the adjacent surface; the foliage is completely self-sufficient. The manifest continuity of the ornament within itself and in its setting is unmistakable in this example.

PILASTER 14

The next example is yet another combination of geometric armature set forth by ribbons or bands that create three equal figures on the face of the impost block (fig. 1.16). Their crossings and extension create Xs bordered top and bottom by foliage that is tightly concentrated and by two mandorlas containing intricate loops and crossings of smaller ribbons. The necking ornament is a somewhat less concentrated leaf form distinct from the planar face of the pilaster. The energy of "imagination," as Sullivan characterizes the development from inorganic to organic, is subdued in this example.

PILASTER 15

The last compound pilaster steps back at the south corner of the entrance wall (fig. 1.17). The impost block face of the double pilaster on the south side is a series of nine vertical forms topped by a spray of leaf-like forms overlapping six swirls of spirals above, creating a syncopated rhythm. The necking at the top of the smooth planes of the pilasters is a band of four spirals wrapped around another spray of foliage distinct from the impost ornament and clearly separate from the pilaster face. The evident geometrical regularity is clearly guided by the principles laid out on Plate 7, "The Value of Parallel Axes."[19] This compositional structure is applicable to any series form, as on this impost block. Referring back to the north double pilaster, we have another series composition of elongated frames closed by arch forms. Within these frames grows an exuberant collection of large leaf forms that aggressively overlap the frames, rising from a flat band behind the frames. The complex layering of geometric frame and overlapping foliage brings to the fore how organic and inorganic cross over. The necking is an almost Gothic interlace of leaves stemming from an offset wave-like pattern, again distinct from the surfaces above and below.

PILASTER 16

The two pilasters next to the entrance doors expand the foliage/mandorla patterns as a demonstration of the interaction of the geometric and the foliate (figs. 2.2 and 2.18). The north pilaster at the entrance repeats six mandorlas with the corner ones bending around to the sides. The flat mandorla frames contain six different foliations running from centered bursts to asymmetrical growth to curved axes that expand over the frame. The bending of motifs around the vertical corners appears again as the sun-ray motifs on the faces of the impost block bend horizontally to the underside and then fold again to the five shield-like panels on the face of the pilaster. This composition of geometric and foliate elements reaches a level of intersection not seen before.

Figure 1.18. Banqueting Hall Pilaster 16.
(© 2000 Nathan Kirkman)

If we look across the room to the parallel pilaster compositions, the contrast between these last geometric patterns and the robust foliated patterns is striking. These amazing and amazingly different examples of ornament show a master designer demonstrating the various ways geometry and foliation, inorganic and organic, enter into dialog. These stunning examples of Sullivan's imagination found in the Auditorium Banqueting Hall ornament explore the interaction between inorganic and organic that he subsequently laid out in the two initial pages of the *A System of Architectural Ornament*.

A SYSTEM OF ARCHITECTURAL ORNAMENT

As presented in the *A System of Architectural Ornament*, this ornamental activity is, of course, an aesthetic exercise, but it is also a conceptual

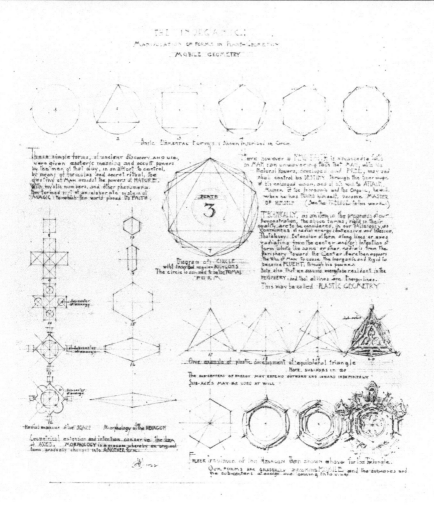

Figure 1.19. "Plate 3" from *A System of Architectural Ornament*, by Louis Sullivan. The Art Institute of Chicago / Art Resource, NY.

exploration.[20] The way organic is contextualized ("contained" and described) by the geometry of the inorganic, and the fact that geometry comes first in Sullivan's *System*, sets a model that Frank Lloyd Wright was sure to have seen as Sullivan laid out the ornament on his drafting board. The *System* is a summation of Sullivan's ornamental activity. It begins with "The Inorganic" (Plate 1), which is "manipulated" "mechanically" to develop "increased Freedom." The origin of the inorganic is found in "the block." The subsequent eleven illustrated stages that unpack the block are immediately recognizable as having direct architectural reference. The use of the term *block* associates it as an element in construction. The effect of practical considerations on *freedom* immediately shows how Sullivan's attention is simultaneously on, shall we say, theory and practice. This correlation of theory and practice sacrifices singular clarity or focus by recognizing the complex boundaries that an architect works between.

After the "Inorganic," the next plate is "Manipulation of the Organic" which is indicated in the "seed form." If manipulation of the inorganic block is an internally framed operation that proceeds in the timeless world of geometry, the leaf and seed forms develop in time, growing and expanding from initial conditions that do not limit but provide potential. This manipulation of the organic begins in a pattern that has geometric roots, and through iteration and subdivision, then expansion, produces elaborate patterns on an initial armature that enables indefinite elaboration. The guidance of geometry even in the development of the organic is a central feature of the *System*.

The next demonstration, Plate 3, is entitled "The Inorganic: Manipulation of Forms in Plane-Geometry. Mobile Geometry" (fig. 1.19). The word *mobile* gives the geometric framework, which begins as static, the potential for expansion without referring to the botanical model. Where the inorganic began in "the block," Sullivan moves to the circle in Plate 3 as the "primal form" whose geometry generates "radial expansion." With the introduction of the radius, geometry becomes mobile, "fluent," energizing the square, triangle, and hexagon. The rigidity of the polygons is liberated as they become "containers of radial energy" through the operation of the will of man. Human contribution to the organic, then, is the abstraction provided by geometry. The development of the triangle and the hexagon in the lower right of the plate shows how this extension becomes "mobile." The initial separation of inorganic and organic is set in motion, made fluid, through the inherent energy of the radial extension and the presence of man's will. Why the organic would need energizing is a puzzle. But the organic is a category of human construction that could, if left alone, stiffen up like pleached fruit trees or a topiary cone. The complex boundary between these two categories as Sullivan presents them in 1924 is what Wright responded to thirty years previously as the basis for his interpretation that ornament could lead to architecture.

The alternation between fluency derived from both geometry and the botanical world is explored in Plate 5, where geometry and the botanical model of the seed form are brought together. The generative axes of geometry, the linear extension of forces, are posed next to the curved, non-Euclidean patterns found in the seed-germ. There is a surprising lack of comment on the seed-germ's sudden, specific appearance; its curves just appear. The force that produces geometric axes seems very different from the force that grows a leaf. The difference may be that one is the result of man's intellect and will, while the other originates in the world of nature. Seeing a parallel between them may be the foundation of an "organic" interpretation of human construction. Further fertile ambiguity appears in Plate 7, where the notes about fluency and infinite variety lead to the graphic exploration of "The Values of Parallel Axes." At the bottom of the plate appears the clearest evidence of the sequence in the development of Sullivan's ornament. The geometric armature is exposed to the right and left of the fully developed foliate pattern. The alternating V-shaped elements embracing a circle are clearly laid down first as a kind of trellis which then supports and guides the foliation. The result indicates Sullivan's mastery of structure and draftsmanship. By drawing the stages he used to create his ornament, he sets down the sequence from inorganic geometry to botanical foliage. This last stage, which follows the armature even as it overcomes it, adds the third dimension to the flat, two-dimensional geometric frame. The magic of this last stage is accomplished by drawing the shadows of the foliate projections beyond the plane of the geometry. Shadows add the directionality of a light source. The planar geometry itself also includes some overlaps tightly bound to the surface. When the foliage is added, projection and recess spring forth. Two dimensions swell into three. The vivid efflorescence of foliate material and the manipulation of geometry are explored further in the rest of Plate 7.

In Plate 4, it is clear that through the will of man, his free choice, intelligence, and skill, but not through botanical mimicry, the inorganic and the organic could be fused. At this point the foliate forms appear. Although Sullivan brings back the seed-germ, all the drawing and notation of geometry has ended up at the same point of fluency, expansion, and growth as that of a plant. Of course, Sullivan is not representing any specific plants. He learned the generic forms of organic life from his likely study in Paris with Ruprich-Robert and certainly from the material in Ruprich-Robert's book, *Flore Ornamental*, along with the illustrations in Gray's *School and Field Book of Botany*. Sullivan is abstracting and conventionalizing plant forms, but geometry accomplishes that in one step. For Sullivan it is the means to achieve that end, not the goal in itself. Geometry is a strange thing. It transcends time and place; the circle is the same for a 2000 BCE Egyptian and for a 20th-century American. And yet it is also a human creation. Geometry seems to straddle nature as non-human and abstract, and as deeply human.

Correlating the Banqueting Hall examples with the *System's* analysis three decades later reveals the continuing interaction of geometry and foliation. The wonderful pencil drawings in the *System* that present the sequence of his process tell us that he began with his drawing instruments to lay out the armature of geometry, not just as a convenience, but as the first step of his description of lines and axes of energy. This structure results in "plastic geometry" as the energy of intensive and extensive paths is realized. The center and the periphery locate this energy and might stand for inductive and deductive reasoning or organism and context. Although Sullivan does not name such parallels, in his explanation of what he is pursuing, he cites philosophical concepts that go beyond the pencil lines he is drawing.

When the geometric description of energy axes is laid out, Sullivan picks up his softer pencil to draw the organic forms. When he does this, something amazing happens: the third dimension and time are introduced. The stability of the two-dimensional armature is animated. What is drawn is the shadow of the third dimension. The apparent light source is almost uniformly from the conventional upper left, but some of the shadows of the smaller scale foliate forms are less directional. The carved Banqueting Hall ornament is, of course, actually three-dimensional, and the energy of the foliation rises up to cast shadows from whatever light source is present in the room. Time is introduced as well by the implication of growth underlying the foliate forms. The variation developed between the inorganic and organic forms shows Sullivan exploring the potential each category presents. The examples of the pilasters where geometry is prominent present more static compositions.

Wright's significant interpretation of ornament goes way beyond Sullivan's discussion in his 1892 essay "Ornament in Architecture."[21] Ten years later, Sullivan reemphasized what he saw as ornament's role in architecture when in *Kindergarten Chats* he wrote, referring to a department store: "No matter about that ornament up there by —. We are a long way from discussing ornament—if ever we discuss it. Ornament, when creative, spontaneous, is a perfume. It is, to change the figure, the smile of sentiment, the last line in the sonnet."[22] Perfume is a long way from what Wright considered the source of the important lesson he said he got from Sullivan's ornament. Perfume is so representative of how the conservative 19th century described ornament; the very tradition that saw ornament as "the garment of poetic imagery" that added "charm," according to Sullivan. In the 1892 essay, Sullivan presented ornament as something to be used to extend what he sees as a building's "nature" as an "emotional expression." What distinguishes Sullivan's sentiment from sentimentality, a distinction Wright often made, is that it is inherently part of the "mass and proportion" of the architecture without ornament that was "well-formed and comely in the nude."[23] In spite of the perfume reference, Sullivan considered ornament as a continuation of the "noble and dignified" "emotional expression" of architecture as a work of art. This "emotional impulse shall flow throughout harmoniously into its varied form of expression—of which, while the mass-composition is the more profound, the decorative ornamentation is the more intense."[24] "A peculiar sympathy between the ornament and the structure" points directly to Wright, but Sullivan does not explore how that sympathy would be established; ornament was still something both separable and somehow connected. One wonders if his facility and delight in his soft-pencil foliage simply obscured what Wright was able to see. Sullivan saw the necessity of a "preparatory basis of what may be called an organic system of ornamentation" and he devoted considerable thought and energy in laying that out three decades later, but it was up to Wright to go the next mile.[25]

"The spirit that animates the mass is free to flow into the ornament—they are no longer two things but one thing."[26] This proposition of Sullivan's has such a familiar ring with Wright's concept of the organic and his method of making his ornament out of the geometric armature rather than picking up Sullivan's soft pencil to draw the foliage. That next step made the creation a two-step process instead of one. Although Wright's architecture is expressive and has emotional sentiment, he combines that impulse with a discipline more intellectual and even mathematical, considering geometry as visible mathematics. When Sullivan begins his *System of Architectural Ornament* with the "Inorganic," he indicates what the basis for the designs is. Wright also began there, but he made the inorganic the head and the heart, the stable and the dynamic, the "simplicity of mind" and the "depth of feeling" as the basis of his architecture as an interpretation of Sullivan's ornament.

Ornament sets up how one considers the relation between two and three dimensions, particularly when looking at Sullivan's ornament. The interaction of two and three dimensions has profound implications for the development of visual patterns, as we have traced, but it also correlates to larger considerations that Sullivan's text in the *A System of Architectural Ornament* makes clear. He makes quite clear how he thinks of patterns in ornamental and intellectual realms as reciprocal. This correlation sets the terms for Wright's subsequent exploration of the connection that he carries to much greater consequence. That expansive correlation suggests to me a connection that might seem initially remote, but I beg your indulgence as I pursue it.

The interaction and relation of two and three dimensions is explored in an essay by the eminent British poet and essayist John Holloway.[27] His probing essay "The Waste Land" identifies what is "modern" in T.S. Eliot's ground-breaking poem published in 1922 and indicates how that modernity relates to Eliot's commitment to tradition, an increasingly important subject for Eliot. In *Mimesis*, Erich Auerbach's compelling review of Western literature, two contrasting terms describe patterns of relationship between words in styles of writing.[28] *Hypotaxis*, subordination, characterizes writing full of dependent clauses. *Parataxis*, placing elements side by side, is more like a list of words equally spaced. Holloway considers the relation of historical practices to contemporary desires. He explores the question whether *The Waste Land* is paratactic or hypotactic. His highly suggestive argument links literary form with graphic form based on the distinction between hypotactic and paratactic composition. He explores the significance of things distributed in a hierarchical composition, e.g., in three dimensions or in perspective compared to a two-dimensional plane. The point of citing this remote example is to give Sullivan's ornament a broader context for interpretation and to expand the philosophical commentary already present in Sullivan's own text that accompanies his drawings in the *System*.

Holloway extends the literary context for hypotaxis and parataxis to the world of modern visual art by correlating it with what he identifies as characteristic of modern poetry circa 1920s.

The juxtaposition, the repetition of "and" substitutes for hypotactic subordination of perspective by means of the paratactic singular plane of the visual world. The "19th century is a delicate tissue of universal inter-relatedness and interweaving…while…our time…is stark juxtaposition, disruption, and discontinuity."[29] The hypotactic 19th century is replaced by the paratactic modern 20th century. "Modern" may be seen as effecting this replacement.

The hypotactic method achieves correlation of literary and visual arts through the word *harmony*. Harmony is not a list, a collection that can be shuffled and rearranged by many external forces. Harmony is inherently hypotactical. Harmony appears in Frank Lloyd Wright's earliest description of what he is trying to achieve in his architecture. Whether Wright is of the 19th or the modern 20th century has been debated by architectural historians. He clearly spans those approaches and that is why his "boundaries" are so complex when he writes explanations or designs buildings. "[Q]uiet thoughtful consistency throughout brings this harmony to be a factor in our daily lives, and it is good for sore eyes and tired nerves," written in 1894 when Wright was twenty-seven.[30]

Holloway's description of visual arts using hypotactic and paratactic categories can be expanded to address the perspective illusion of depth that is replaced by or stopped at the picture plane itself. The modernist project brings all the three-dimensional subjects of perspective up to the two-dimensional surface. What this amounts to is the replacement of three dimensions by two. The only directions of movement in paratactic space are across the two dimensions of a flat plane. Hypotactic space is navigated perpendicularly. It connects the "here" and "there" through complex three dimensional layering that a flat plane cannot provide.

Visual subjects in the paratactic world are simply adjacent to each other; in the hypotactic world, they are arranged in perspective according to a priority of what is near and what is far, what is primary and what is subordinate. One can imagine that the rules that subordinated interrelatedness would eventually come under increased scrutiny as values changed. Modernism could be seen to reject subordinating elements according to the received convention by making them a "list." By bringing those subjects up to a two-dimensional plane they could be examined potentially for rearrangement in a new hypotactic system, or, more radically, left on the plane as a continuing protest to any subordinating structure. One explanation for this radical revaluing is that subordination is, by definition, oppression. Relationships should always be free and fluid. In the interest of such freedom, the potential for relationship is restricted to what can be achieved on the plane of two dimensions. The adjacency is controlled even as it is limited. In spatial terms, when, say, inside and out are posed simply as adjacencies with no contact except on the two-dimensional plane, there is only opposition, only stark difference. Nuance or complexity are impossible. With the addition of the third dimension, these possibilities are amplified.

The third dimension has a central place in Frank Lloyd Wright's conception of architecture. How much it was on his mind is testified to by a story Philip Johnson related in a panel at the Jewish Museum in New York in November 1963. He remembered a moment when he and Wright were passing through a door in Venice. Wright tapped his cane on the walls of the short passage and said to Johnson: "Philip, the third dimension!" Johnson recalled this event precisely because he knew how revelatory it was of Wright's architecture. The third dimension was the connection, the perpendicular, between one condition or place and another. It is the crucial "third term" required for effective analysis of and connection between two categories. It is crucial that Wright pointed out the third dimension while moving through it. The third dimension takes time to move both body and eye forward and back beyond the flat plane of the present. Holloway's essay points out what is missing in parataxis's static singularity; human experience of movement in time.

Wright addresses the third dimension directly in the essay by that name in the *Wendingen* journal in 1925.[31] This essay is identified as one of the essays comprising the series "In the Cause of Architecture," first published in the *Architectural Record* beginning in 1908, but the "Third Dimension" essay was presented for the first time in the Dutch journal. In this essay Wright harkens back to the "Art and Craft of the Machine" lecture he presented twenty-four years earlier where he characterizes the "new art" as form having "the new plastic sense...the plastic ideal" that enters with the third dimension.[32] With this further synthesis of plasticity and the third dimension, "the laboriously made aggregation in two dimensions gives way to the unity born of conditions—plastic now— the third dimension essential to its reality." Wright cites Unity Temple as an example of how the third dimension comes into play when he says: "A sense of the third dimension in the use of the 'box' and the 'slab'—and a sense of the room within as the thing to be expressed in arranging them are what made Unity Temple; instead of the two-dimension-sense of the traditional block mass sculptured into architectural form from without."[33] Its plasticity led Cornelius van de Ven to define "that phenomenon quite remarkably as the 'three-dimensional.'"[34] For Wright to see the "box" and the "slab" as three-dimensional while the "block mass" is not presents a complicated definition of three-dimensionality. He had tried to explain this conundrum two years earlier when he was writing about the Imperial Hotel in Tokyo: "I am not one of those who conceive of a building as a carved and sculpted block of building material. That is two-dimension thinking"[35] (fig. 1.20).

Trying to unpack this tantalizing conception, one is led to the possibility that the block is inert. It shares the static quality of two dimensions. Its planar surfaces can only be "carved and sculpted" because they cannot expand into the third dimension. I admit Wright's description remains elusive, but the way the third dimension is activated means it must rise away from a surface much like Sullivan's ornament.

Figure 1.20. Surviving portion of Frank Lloyd Wright's Imperial Hotel, now in Inuyama, Japan. (Photo by Sidney K. Robinson)

Flat ornament completely generated from plane geometry is bereft of the central constituents of time and space. Hypotactic ornament, i.e., Sullivan's, led Wright to hypotactic architecture by animating geometry off the plane into the third dimension. Wright's interpretive leap was to follow Sullivan's interaction of inorganic and organic by giving geometry the hypotactic dimension usually ascribed to the organic. This may be one way to come to terms with Wright's "fuzzy," or "slippery" meaning of that iconic word *organic*. It was always an apparently unstable combination of nature and man; nature "out there," and nature in man's head. It was never biomimicry. If we follow the evolution of Wright's interpretation of ornament into architecture beginning with Sullivan's example, the astonishing move Wright made was to take Sullivan's synthesis much further. If Sullivan prioritized inorganic in the sequence of his plates, Wright picked up that category and, rather than putting down his T-square and triangle to pick up the foliating soft pencil, he made geometry do the whole job: flat armature expanded into three-dimensional architecture. The result is organic of a very subtle kind.

To bracket what *organic* might mean to Wright, let's consider two iconic designs five years apart. The first is Unity Temple (1905–1907), discussed above. It is the clearest example of organic as an integrated nesting of geometric and spatial patterns of surface, volume, and ornament. Tightly strung on axes, symmetry, and compositional hierarchy, Unity Temple is a brilliant, abstract architectural conclusion with traditional architectural models; clear, harmonious, and resolved, at least in its geometry of construction if not the radical departure of the interior! As an example of the sequence leading to resolution, the ornament on the short columns at the top of the walls in front of the leaded glass began as naturalistic branches with stylized leaves. The resolution came when the dominant orthogonal geometry brought the branches into geometric alignment with the whole composition.

Taliesin (1911–1959) is another kind of organic. From the beginning Wright knew that his evolving activity professionally and personally would take place in the flow of time. Even as he was beginning construction of Taliesin, he was drawing up expanded facilities for residences and studio spaces. It was changing even as it began, a direction, but not a conclusion. Taliesin is an organism that adapted over time. The way Wright maintained its identity with change built-in is a singular architectural achievement. Because there are only hints of axes and symmetries, their interruption does not draw attention to them. The major continuity is the set of materials whose relationships are maintained even as that relationship evolves. Limestone, wood, plaster, are all malleable; their "nature" is not fixed, unconditioned by their context. Alternatively, Unity Temple is a conceptual organic of abstract resolution. Taliesin is a life; an organic of temporal evolution. Both of these aspects, like Sullivan's *inorganic* and *organic,* are central to Wright's embrace of the complex boundary between them.

When Wright continues developing his ornament by using the geometric tools on his drafting board rather than picking up a soft pencil, he is collapsing the distinction between geometry and botanical imagery, between inorganic and organic patterns. His reinterpretation of the organic activates the boundary between geometry and botanical specifics by recognizing that the organic has within it a distinction between underlying structure—geometry—and the immediate patterns represented by Sullivan's soft pencil drawing. Organic becomes a single category with an internal boundary: organic now consists of geometry in two functions, as armature and as visual pattern. That is the key demonstration of his understanding of continuity and plasticity. The potential of geometry as armature, as underlying structure is combined with its potential to create the immediate patterns that Sullivan had added as foliage. This boundary condition sets up new crossovers where *organic* as visual patterns and *inorganic* as structural armature are viewed alternatively from their respective realms. These alternating perspectives together create a continuity of perception that led Wright to combine structure with delight.

Frank Lloyd Wright took Sullivan's system and built a whole new way to relate ornament and architecture, not by erasing the differences between the two categories, but by seeing each from the perspective of the other. This interpretive leap saw differences as energizing; continuity and plasticity not only applicable to ornament, but to architecture as well. Wright's interpretive power is the consequence of crossing the boundaries between inorganic and organic, between ornament and architecture, and between continuity and plasticity. By seeing those categories as reciprocal, not oppositional, by seeing one from the perspective of the other, his buildings and his commentary are never static; they are energized by multiple perspectives. Sullivan's essays on ornament took place in a world of design and architecture that explored the status of ornament in fertile and contradictory ways. Now we will review how ornament was discussed around the turn of the 20th century insofar as the concepts and terms inform how we consider what Sullivan and Wright were exploring in their respective work.

CHAPTER TWO

COMMENTARY ON ORNAMENT BY WRIGHT AND HIS HISTORICAL CONTEXT

F rank Lloyd Wright's conception of how ornament could be related to architecture is different from discussions of ornament before and after the turn of the 20th century. While others were arguing whether ornament should look one way or another, whether it should be based on abstract patterns or naturalistic illustrations, Wright was thinking about it from a very different perspective: how its abstract composition could inform whole buildings. The comments on ornament outlined here are not presented as a history but as background to point up how distinct was Wright's conception of ornament's potential to lead to architecture.

Ornament, surprisingly, provided a significant subject to address the impact industrialization had on art and architecture. Ornament traditionally appeared in two major sites: craft and art. With industrialization, mechanized production of ornament became a threat to both sites. The conflict in both craft and art centered around the question: should ornament be abstract or naturalistic? It would make a difference if ornament could influence architecture or architecture could influence ornament. Art Nouveau's sinuous curves affected the architecture of windows and doors, stairs and structure. The ornament on the short columns at Wright's Unity Temple (1905–1907) began as naturalistic, stylized branches and leaves but he soon brought the ornament into alignment with the orthogonal geometry of the building with the line of small rectangles we see today. Rather than the ornament leading the architecture, here we have the building leading the ornament. Wright characterized that sequence as "integral ornament," a proposition that he stressed repeatedly, of course, but one that did not settle the issue for him. He was to go beyond the appearance of ornament by seeing how ornament could lead to architecture at a conceptual rather than a formal level.

In the 19th century, arguments for naturalistic ornament had the backing of the tradition of representational art that conveyed a subject or argument. Before the extreme denigration of ornament by the Modern movement, Western architectural conventions valued the contributions patterns could make to the architectural whole. Pattern, by adding symbolism and formal elaboration to abstract, architectural form, directed attention beyond architecture as a construction of materials and function to issues of perception and signification.

Natural forms had long been adapted for architectural ornamentation by means of conventionalization: Egyptian papyrus and Greek acanthus as tops of columns, for example. Although opposing naturalistic to abstract set up an extreme distinction, employing conventionalization crossed over the difference between the two categories by applying geometric abstraction to natural phenomena. It provided a historical basis for moving toward abstraction. And although that approach had detractors like John Ruskin, its advocates cited economics, science, the process of construction, and theory to bolster their substitution of geometry for naturalism.

John Ruskin (1819–1900), the eminent Victorian critic, held fast to nature as the model for ornament for compositional reasons but also for a moral foundation. He saw the life of nature and human nature not as systematic, but as variable based on his sensitive, close observation of their unique examples. Ruskin's delight and focus on the details of nature are evident in his beautiful drawings of flowers, rocks, plants. For him "precision equaled inhumanity; unique, inconsistent, and unpredictable traits, on the other hand, provide evidence of life."[36] Order and its concomitant generalization of both social and aesthetic examples conflicted with the value of human life. It is not so surprising that Ruskin hated the geometry of the Alhambra for its perfection and repose.[37] His delight in spontaneous details may also explain his estimation of the value of the Gothic. We know Wright read Ruskin, but on the matter of the Gothic, he was clearly at odds with Ruskin's assertion: "Do not try...to connect the delight which you take in ornament with that which you take in construction and usefulness. They have no connection."[38]

Ruskin's position limited ornament's potential for abstract development by focusing on the appearance of the natural world. While Ruskin loved drawing the variation in the details of Gothic buildings, it was not its details but its system of structure and order that held Wright's attention. That view was more aligned with his reading of the French architect and author Eugene Viollet-le-Duc (1814–1879). Wright's interest in seeing across categorical boundaries immediately reminds us that the structural system of the Gothic was not bare and abstract; its system was conveyed by the linear network of moldings, colonettes, and ribs that was simultaneously structure and ornament. This may be a clue to Wright's repeated citation of the Gothic as a history worth noticing as opposed to the Renaissance! ("The setting sun all Europe mistook for dawn," a quote from Victor Hugo that Wright used his whole life.) The suggestive uncertainty between ornament and structure in the Gothic appears again in the 20th century when ornament escaped the boundaries of conventional definition as observed by the historian Julius Meier-Graefe in the architecture of artist/architect Henri van de Velde: "One is unsure where the pure structure ends and the ornament begins."[39]

The search for support of abstraction as the basis for ornament in contrast to natural models was taken up by many designers and historians in the later 19th and early 20th centuries. The resistance to displacing naturalistic models, in addition to Ruskin's moral commitments, was a reaction to the effect that industrialization was having on design. Ruskin observed that "...stylization of nature into geometric figures produced 'conventional uniformity.'"[40] When stylization was linked to mechanization, when the value of geometric pattern was undermined by the easy repetition of mechanization, supporters of abstraction had to argue that their goals were separate from the association with industrialization. The overlap of geometric conventionalization and the "typical" produced by industrial methods suggested to some that the evolution of ornament toward abstraction led to its own demise as mechanism overcame art.

The confusion over ornament's role and appearance in the 19th century led to outright rejection in the 20th century with the rhetoric of Modernism. In a strangely familiar way, Ruskin's morality supported the ascetic cleansing Modernism advocated. Ornament's multiplicity has often been seen as a distraction from the plainness of truth. That proposition recreated the perennial purifying motivation that appears in 17th-century English literature's "plain style" that sought to clarify language by avoiding figures of speech and Bernard of Clairvaux's Cistercian purification of the Cluniac's efflorescence of ornament in architecture and music in the 12th century. (More than one vocal line meant the message of the text was no longer singular.) Modernism itself can be construed as a puritanical effort to scrape off the excesses, signified by ornament, of Victorian and Queen Anne predecessors.

In spite of all the theorizing and commentary that sought to reinterpret the role of ornament around the turn of the 20th century, the advent of Modernism cut off further investigation by simply banning it altogether, or so the rhetoric would suggest. Following on from the Austrian architect/commentator Adolf Loos's lecture, published in 1913, where he asserted "Ornament as Crime," the exhibition of Modern Decorative and Industrial Arts in Paris, 1925, characterized ornament as fatally distracting and likely debilitating. The trivialization of ornament by mechanical repetition was one excuse, but more importantly, vanquishing 19th-century confusion required strong, clear action to build the new world of design and ultimately of society.

Ornament was not considered separable from social/cultural conditions; it was symptomatic and circumstantial. It could not be saved by calls for abstraction to supplant naturalism. Its superficiality, its application to more substantial and serious work not only did not add anything important, it distracted from efforts to instill design with morality. Henry Russell Hitchcock and Philip Johnson made ornament anathema in their ground-breaking exhibition in 1932 at the Museum of Modern Art in New York City, "Modern Architecture: International Exhibition." They announced "the elimination of any kind of ornament and artificial pattern. This lack of ornament is one of the most difficult elements of the style for the layman to accept. Intrinsically there is no reason why ornament should not be used, but modern ornament, usually crass in design and machine-manufactured, would seem to mar rather than adorn the lean perfection of surface and proportion."[41] They explicitly called out the failure of Frank Lloyd Wright to get with the program by observing: "Midway Gardens [is] an expansion of Wright's architecture in a decorative direction which had been repressed since his early work with Sullivan."[42] Since the middle of the preceding century, ornament had to fight on two fronts; it had to claim relevance by proposing abstraction as the method to escape naturalism and at the same time argue that abstraction was not to be confused with mechanical repetition. Ornament's vulnerability to dismissal from both sides made it easy simply to reject it out of hand.

Industry in nineteenth century Britain operated, not on theory, but on economy. Its processes aligned more effectively with abstraction than naturalism. William Dyce (1806–1864), painter and educator at the new School of Design at Somerset House in London, made significant contributions to the discussion of how nature and abstraction could be related. The very title of the school challenges the traditional artistic practice of naturalist imitation by proposing the abstraction implied by "design." According to Debra Schafter's estimable *The Order of Ornament, the Structure of Style*, "The inability of British manufacturers to produce technically naturalistic qualities created by foreign designers led reformers to establish geometric formality as the basis of 'fit' ornament."[43] Schafter's use of the word *reformers* locates the activity in the larger context of economic and industrial changes. Although Dyce's book "Drawing-book of the School of Design" in 1842–43 conceded that nature must be held up as the model for direct imitation, he was willing to go significantly further toward geometric abstraction in his ornamental principles:

"ornamental art is rather abstractive and reproductive than imitative."[44] The School of Design "argued that neither the designer nor the creator of decorative patterns should copy the pictorial aspect of the products of nature, but rather should try to identify their general structure and conventional abstraction."[45]

While Ruskin speaks for ornament having an unbreakable connection to naturalism, Dyce's 1843 book presented a growing interest in not approaching ornament exclusively from a naturalistic perspective. This interest was expressed by many designers and theorists. When ornament came to be seen as an abstract pattern, it overcame its naturalistic limitations. The British author Ralph Wornum, keeper of the National Gallery, in his 1850 book *Analysis of Ornament* linked ornament and music: "the analogy between music and ornament [is] perfect: one is to the eye what the other is to the ear....[E]very correct ornamental scheme is a combination...or a measured succession of forms...called in the first counterpoint, and in the other symmetrical contrast."[46] Music became a prominent analogy to support abstract ornament as a contribution to architecture. Gottfried Semper (1803–1879), German architect, author, and professor, proposed in his 1856 "Theory of Formal Beauty" that architecture can be grouped, not just as a plastic art, but "with dance and music as a 'cosmic art'—cosmic because their laws of spatial harmony are immanently form giving, decorative in the very manipulation of their basic elements."[47] Because music, as understood in the 19th century, was composed with lawful structure, it served as an important reference to elevate and guide abstract ornamental design.

If ornament, as Semper posited, was the natural result of materials and processes, architecture followed from ornament's influence. Although few followed Semper's model, it opened up a direction of agency of ornament to architecture that Wright may have considered. There has been some suggestion that Semper's views could have been known in Chicago architectural circles through the presence of John Edelmann in the office of Adler and Sullivan. Edelmann had secondary contact with Leopold Eidlitz, architect and author, who proposed a form of "organic" ideas akin to Semper. Eidlitz's book, *The Nature and Function of Art, More Especially of Architecture* (1881), contributed to his large discussion of ornament and architecture. This citation is not presented to show that Wright knew about Semper. Wright's exploration of what ornament could contribute to architecture, and architecture could contribute to ornament, took place in a context of concepts and terms focused on this issue.[48]

Ornament was drawn into the changes occurring not only of mechanization and national economies, but as an element in the new attention designers were paying to science. The category of "organic design," as it came to be called, was initiated by the rise of the life sciences in the early 19th century. Geometric abstraction described the forces of physics—light and gravity—but it was also useful in categorizing patterns seen in all sorts of living organisms. It provided the same tool for diagramming abstract structure of natural phenomena as it did for "natural philosophy," or physics. Describing and categorizing natural phenomena relied on visual conventions found in geometric patterns. William Dyce's curriculum in the School of Design connected ornamental design with science's formal categories used by botanical analysis by including classes in chemistry and botany in addition to the traditional subjects of life drawing, perspective, painting, and sculpture.[49]

Gottfried Semper wrote in an 1852 letter that the explorations of the life sciences could provide patterns useful for designers: "When I observed this variety of nature in its simplicity, I very often thought by myself that it may be possible to reduce the creations of man and especially the works of architecture, to certain normal and elementary forms, which, in a comparing method of contemplating them, analogous to that of Curvier for natural history."[50] The citation of Georges Cuvier, French naturalist and zoologist (1769–1832), brings up a significant controversy in the way to understand biological nature. The famous argument in Paris in 1830 between Cuvier and French naturalist Geoffroy Saint-Hilaire (1772–1844) posed two descriptions of the origins for the forms that natural organisms took. Geoffroy posited that the parts were outgrowths of the whole, while Cuvier saw the whole evolved from the parts.[51]

This distinction holds significant implications for any design discipline. Should the compositional whole be determined by the shared characteristic of the parts, or should the character of the whole align the parts? On one level the distinction between abstract and naturalistic bases for ornament poses the same question: naturalism focuses on the specific and abstraction unifies the whole. Biology began with the struggle to say what constitutes an identifiable part when it inextricably functioned in a complex, organic whole. Nearly a hundred years later in America, this difference led Edward Stuart Russell in "Form and Function" (1916) to observe: "The contrast between the teleological attitude, with its insistence on the priority of function to structure, and the morphological attitude, with its conviction of the priority of structure to function, is one of the more fundamental in biology. Cuvier and Geoffroy are the greatest representatives of these opposing views."[52]

An American effort to promote abstract design appeared in architectural education in the 1890s. "Denman W. Ross [*The Theory of Pure Design* (1907)], an instructor in design theory at Harvard, and Arthur Dow, an artist and instructor at Pratt and later Teacher's College, Columbia University, devised Pure Design for art education and appreciation."[53] Exercises were based on elements of dots, lines, shapes, and color that created abstract compositions demonstrating general principles of harmony, balance, and rhythm. Their efforts clearly extended Friedrich Froebel's practice decades earlier that educated kindergartners to combine and manipulate geometric materials. The continuity of interest in finding ways to make designs from bases other than historical examples, representations of nature, or artifacts that aimed at verisimilitude correlated with the ongoing programs to connect ornament to larger entities.

Calling on biological science to support the replacement of naturalism by abstraction is further evidence that ornament was engaging many sources to provide it with a foundation separate from adventitious appearance. Lawfulness gave ornament a whole new standing. The life science references are the basis for the subsequent identification of design as "organic." The interrelatedness of the parts of organic life was a powerful model to guide the compositions of design. Here form, not imitative form, but lawful form, applied to ornament bestowed a seriousness that imitation could not match. Organic was applied to, of all things, Greek architecture by Gottfried Semper who saw the Hellenic "aim in animating the architectural parts themselves instead of decorating them with ornamental applications."[54] Applied forms were not integral, were not aligned with the structure of natural examples, they were extraneous, the very condition advocates of lawful ornament sought to overcome.

Nature as a reference for the design of ornament preserved its traditional place, but to displace it from its primary status by proposing that the details of its appearance be subsumed to a geometric pattern overturned the hierarchy of history. Close attention to the appearance of nature, however, had initiated biological investigations to describe categories of phenomena. Descriptions of what appeared in the natural world uncovered things that looked similar and things that looked different: parts or wholes or contexts. How a thing looked depended on what you were looking for. When descriptions led to categorization, the specifics of appearance stepped back behind abstract geometry. Owen Jones's (1809–1874) important *The Grammar of Ornament* (1856) saw abstraction as the means to relate ornament to natural forms. However, Jones still constrained ornament's role by cautioning: "Although ornament is most properly only an accessory to architecture [it] should never be allowed to usurp the place of structural feature."[55]

When Jones published his *Grammar of Ornament*, he opened up the range of examples beyond the Western canon to include Egyptian and Persian ornament. The support for this extension was the result of "certain general laws [that] appear to reign independently of the individual peculiarities of each [style]."[56] Various sources were sought to give the abstraction of naturalist images structure. The most available source were the conventions of Euclidian geometry. Regular figures, symmetry, and axes were immediate references that could be laid over the variations of natural objects. To counter charges that ornament was whimsical and wayward, the discipline of geometry provided the lawfulness.

Technical processes of making ornament also supplied lawful guides. The construction of a building, the materials, the means of assemblage and production obey certain obvious patterns of composition that could not be breached. Gottfried Semper, who had spent time in Henry Cole's Department of Practical Art in London beginning in 1832, pointed out how the handling of materials enforced rules: "...inherent lawfulness that...technical processes impose on form-making [defines] architecture in its essence as an *ornamental* activity."[57] Here is a very early correlation between ornament and architecture that resulted from a newly extended definition of ornament based on its origin in the way materials were handled.

When materials are being manipulated directly, their "nature," to quote Wright, suggests ways to elaborate their inherent capabilities to produce form. Mechanical processes, however, made it possible to manipulate materials by overriding their natures. The impulse to go beyond mere construction, whether instigated by extra resources or desire to make something expressive of the craftsperson's skill, can result in making the material, say in architectural construction of brick, stone, or wood, ornamental. This basis ensures that the ornament has direct connection to the constructional and material context from which it grows. Of course, craftspersons who are exposed to art and aspire to be recognized for their knowledge of art can include references to that world to distinguish their work by using naturalistic patterns. Ornament that is designed by an artist inevitably includes references and precedents beyond its material basis. The handling of material can have a more abstract, less figurative result owing to concentration on the potentials and limitations of the material itself. This abstraction also has a measure of economy because its content is not "imported" but indigenous.

Wright's capacity to interpret formal patterns beyond their appearance in order to find their functional, and even symbolic, potential is what led him to see how abstract ornament could lead to architecture. Richard MacCormac's insightful 1968 essay, "The Anatomy of Wright's Aesthetic," names a prominent pattern in Wright's architecture and planning: the tartan grid.[58] How Wright came to see the potential of this pattern is not recoverable, but we can identify its appearance in very early Western architecture. It is evident in Greek megarons and classical temples: a wide, main space is flanked by narrow spaces which also characterize the basilicas of Roman legal buildings. (One might imagine extending this ubiquitous pattern into section and elevation as base and capital or crown molding correlate to the smaller elements bracketing the extent of the column or wall.) It is the narrow-wide-narrow pattern of Roman, monumental gates, churches (nave and side aisles), and palaces. What Wright does is take this figural plan and transform it into a field or grid for planning purposes. He uses it to compose entries, service and served spaces, as well as for structure. Here we have a pattern that appears in construction, is transformed into an ornamental grid, and reappears as a spatial, functional, structural pattern for a 20th-century American architect. Although turning the figure into a field can be seen as a modern transformation, it remains a hierarchical pattern. If the tartan grid helps organize plans, Wright concurrently uses a unit grid as a guide for construction. The tartan grid with its resonance in figural convention, and the unit grid with its uninflected field, which was also used in historical practice, have been set in opposition by the contemporary critic Rosalind Krauss: "The absolute stasis of the grid, its lack of hierarchy, of center, of inflection, emphasizes not only its anti-referential character, but—more importantly—its hostility to narrative."[59] After

Wright acquires his bona fides in his chosen profession as seen in the Oak Park Studio practice, he is freer to loosen the conventional pattern in the Usonian examples where the tartan grid nearly disappears. Wright dispensed with the tartan grid in favor of the convenient constructional unit grid he had typically used. The freedom to lay out a plan by disposing walls, openings, and structure on a field of equal squares, rectangles, and eventually triangles allowed Wright to create a new spatial hierarchy without historical roots.

Ernst Gombrich's comprehensive review of ornament from a perceptual basis in *The Sense of Order* (1984) sets up a consideration that makes expansion beyond appearance almost inevitable. This expansion is clearly presented when he writes: "The arrangement of elements according to similarity and difference and the enjoyment of repetition and symmetry extend...to the rhythms of movement, speech and music, not to mention the structure of society and the systems of thought."[60] When Gombrich proposes that the category of ornament as decorative design can be opened up to include much larger matters, he is indicating how ornamental composition can be abstracted to include concepts of architecture as Frank Lloyd Wright demonstrated.

The potentials opened up by applying abstraction to ornament went far beyond visual patterns. When the study of ornament came to be a lesson in visual composition, organizing the part with the whole led to applying its lessons to society, or even the universe. As Lada Hubatova-Vackova proposed in her enlightening review, *Silent Revolutions in Ornament*, "ornament should, in its compressed form, demonstrate the unifying idea of higher principles."[61]

Ornament around the turn of the 20th century became the site for significant commentary on the direction its design should take. Displacing naturalism by abstraction opened up new ways to relate ornament to many other activities. The justification for pursuing those new ways was animated by the desire to make integral what had traditionally been added decoration. As the preceding review revealed, many designers and commentators advocated the substitution of abstraction for naturalism. What Frank Lloyd Wright did was abstract even further by applying lessons learned in the creation of ornament to buildings as a whole.

WRIGHT'S WRITING ON ORNAMENT

Wright's references to ornament are surprisingly few before he is sixty as he searched for ways to explain how he interpreted Sullivan's ornament, not for specific formal models but for "structural implications." This reticence to discuss conventional ornament occurred while he produced prodigious amounts of it for buildings and publications. Wright's radical interpretation of Sullivan's ornament, finally laid out in *Genius and the Mobocracy*, took abstraction beyond visual patterns to categories that could structure a whole building. Presumably to combat Modernism's rejection of ornament culminating in the 1932 International Architecture exhibit, he intensified his advocacy for "integral ornament." Curiously these explicit references to ornament occurred as he included less of it compared to his earlier buildings. By now, because he had fully integrated his revolutionary interpretation of ornament's potential to lead to architecture, further examination was no longer needed. The following review of Wright's earlier discussion of ornament concentrates on the ways he avoids conventional expectations for ornament as he tries to explain how ornament led to his architecture.

Imagine what is required to spend as much time as Wright spent on designing ornament and then say virtually nothing about it when he turned to writing about architecture and sometimes about buildings. Something is going on; absence can be as important as presence.

Wright can dismiss ornament by referring to "Jim Crow ornament that makes the whole thing a meaningless freak." What "Jim Crow" ornament might be escapes me, but the talented and knowledgeable Eric O'Malley suggested that Wright might be referring to a rail-bender that turns something straight into a curve.[62] On the other hand, Wright could be seeing how ornament's captivity completely obscured the potential he unleashes.[63] In 1900 when he was 33 and at the beginning of the flowering of work in the Oak Park Studio, he refers to architectural ornament as having the potential to refer to architecture in an abstract way. The possibilities for ornament laid out in the preceding review of concepts and terms raises questions: Is its subject nature? Is it an example? Is it to be imitated in a naturalistic way? What is an architect to do with it? Wright expands on these questions: "A work of Architecture is a great coordination with a distinct and vital organism, but it is in no sense naturalistic—it is the highest, most subjective, conventionalization of Nature known to man, and at the same time it must be organically true to nature when it is really a work of Art." Here is another instance of Wright stating a response only to correct a potential misunderstanding—natural leads to conventional, but not to naturalistic. He continues: "To go back to the lotus of the Egyptians (we may see in these mere details of Art the whole principle), if Egypt had plucked the flower as it grew and had given us merely an imitation of it in stone, it would have died with the original—but turning it into stone and fitting it to grace a column capital, the Egyptian artist put it through a rare and difficult process, wherein its natural character was really revealed and intensified in terms of stone, gaining for it an imperishable significance, for the Life principle of the flower is translated to terms of building stone to satisfy the ideal of a real 'need.'"[64] These observations have few parallels in contemporary discourse.

Wright also describes the Greek conventionalization of the acanthus leaf as a similar lesson in translating nature for architectural purposes. He significantly does not use the word *ornament* to describe these examples. It's as if using that word would be a distraction back into convention and would block the possibility of learning something beyond appearance from the example being described. The citation of specific, plant-based examples places the observation clearly within the traditional context of architectural ornament. The reference is limited to the role of nature in the creation of architecture. When Wright uses the word *ornament* in his discussion of what he learned from Sullivan, he is referring to a vastly different level of abstraction having to do with "structure" in composition and function. His reluctance to refer to ornament in his own architecture is striking and may signal a reasonable fear of being misunderstood. That fear may explain the habit of crossing over boundaries to escape being pigeon-holed.

In "The Art and Craft of the Machine" (1901), there is no reference to ornament, a surprising absence since the effect of the machine on the form and production of ornament was a major issue as the preceding review of historical commentary indicates. Later that year he admits: "Just what this ingrained human love of ornament is, is not clear—not yet."[65] The uncertainty of its effect is significant; it is a subject with too many facets, it would seem. "The time-honored love of ornament" could not be avoided completely, however. Wright saw how the formal contribution of small-scale compositions could be admitted if it came from nature: "As an added grace in summer, foliage and flowers are arranged as a decorative feature of the design, the only ornamentation."[66]

"This use of natural foliage and flowers for decoration is carried to quite an extent in all the designs and, although the buildings are complete without this efflorescence, they may be said to blossom with the season. What architectural decoration the buildings carry is not only conventionalized to the point where it is quiet and stays as a sure foil for the nature of forms from which it is derived and with which it must intimately associate, but it is always *of* the surface never *on* it."[67] This passage from Wright's 1908 *Architectural Record* essay "In the Cause of Architecture" testifies to this major essay's importance as Wright steps onto the national professional stage. He clearly worked to get the message presenting a new way to think about and do architecture right.

In this 1908 presentation, Wright explicitly addresses ornament as the convention of small-scale formal parts of architecture. He suspends any further consideration of how he creates ornament by saying it is so important that it would take too much time to go into now. "To elucidate this element [ornamentation] in composition would mean a long story and perhaps a tedious one, though to me it is the most fascinating phase of the work, involving the true poetry of conception."[68] That curtailment of further discussion is an important indication of how much it meant to him and how only detailed discussion would make his point and avoid misunderstanding. Twenty-five years later in the Kahn Lectures, he defers yet again: "...in numerous ways too tedious to describe in words, this revolutionary sense of the plastic whole, an instinct with me at first, began to work more and more intelligently and have fascinating, unforeseen consequences."[69] Is Wright trying to avoid giving away secrets or is he hesitating because he is, himself, not quite able to put into words the multidimensional consequences of his insight?

His presentation clearly says how integral composition, a way of conceiving formal activity, encompasses every aspect of the design. Working to bring all scales into harmony, to see small elements, usually thought of as something added, conceived as constituent parts of the whole makes the word *ornamentation* inappropriate and seriously misleading. Hence his reluctance to take it up in this 1908 essay. He goes on to describe how a "single, certain simple form...[is] derived and held well together in scale and character...so that each building aesthetically is cut from one piece of goods [a textile reference] and consistently hangs together with an integrity impossible otherwise."[70]

A few paragraphs later, Wright assures us that the conventional reading of ornament is not applicable to what he is trying to build. "We crave ornament for the sake of ornament; cover up our faults of design with ornamental sensualities....[T]he ornamentation of a building should be constitutional, a matter of the nature of the structure beginning with the ground plan." Lest we imagine his buildings bare and raw he assures us that the delight in "richness" and "incident" is not missing, but they are not to be found in "applied decoration, they are found in the fashioning of the whole."[71] This habit we have encountered before: an observation or statement is immediately qualified to displace conventional misunderstanding.

With respect to historical examples of ornament, aside from the specific citation of Egyptian lotus and Greek acanthus, Wright lists very unclassical locations: Mongolian, Indian, Arab, Egyptian, and Gothic. He goes on to list other sources from Japanese artists (Hokusai, Korin), and European examples (Velazquez, Frans Hals), and the repeatedly cited Gothic architecture. In fact, in the 1910 Wasmuth German publisher's folio *Ausgeführte Bauten*, Gothic or Goths are mentioned 14 times, in conjunction with, of all things, Japan. "…the Gothic spirit…organic in character" is not to be used as examples of form. It is the spirit.[72] "A training of this sort [the nature of materials, of the tools and processes, and the nature of the thing they are to be called upon to do] was accorded the great artists of Japan. Although it was not intellectually self-conscious, I have no doubt the apprenticeship of the Middle Ages wrought like results."[73]

Following comments on ornament in the 1908 "In the Cause of Architecture" essay, the introduction to the monumental Wasmuth folio makes limited reference to ornament. In these two major statements of Wright's comprehensive account of his architecture, ornament gets addressed, almost by necessity, anticipating the expectations of the wider audience who would see his work in a national and global context. In the German portfolio ornament is covered this way: "I believe, too, that much ornament in the old sense is not for use yet: we have lost its significance, and I do not believe in adding enrichment merely for the sake of enrichment. Unless it adds clearness to the enunciation of the theme, it is undesirable, for it is very little understood. I wish to say also, what is more to the point, that, in a structure conceived in the organic sense, the ornamentation is conceived in the very ground plan, and is of the very construction of the structure. What ornamentation may be found added purely as such in this structure is thus a makeshift or a confession of weakness or failure."[74]

It is clear Wright is holding out for a new status for ornament, not as an embarrassing evidence of failure, nor as simply enrichment. Tying ornament into the weft and warp of the concept of the integral renders it essential, a difficult challenge he has not quite met. When he worries that "it is very little understood," he is indicating that there is a lot more on his mind than he is willing to take up in these essays.

The most striking absence in Wright's consideration of ornament is found in his extensive report on the Imperial Hotel in Tokyo. In 1990 the Phoenix Art Museum mounted a major exhibit from the Frank Lloyd Wright Archives including drawings of the ornament for the Hotel. It was overwhelming in its intensity of sheer design imagination and the obvious time and effort it took to produce this efflorescence. That visual intensity is striking in contrast to the virtual silence on the subject when Wright writes about the Hotel. "The third material, which was the plastic material used to articulate and decorate the structure, was a lava which I found was used as the ordinary "stone" of the region....The edges of the projecting reinforced concrete slabs were all faced with this lava. The cornices or eaves are all projecting floor or roof slabs, perforated, faced with lava, and interlaced with copper."[75] That is all! One wonders why this reluctance to say more when there is so much more to be seen. In a later discussion of the Hotel he comes as close as he ever does in describing the experience of the architecture and its ornament: "Light and shade play lovingly with the patterned, fretted, overhanging cornices, sifting patterned sun splashes on sturdy walls, tempering but not obstructing the light. A true and simple gaiety. No other building seems to have this charming grace caught from foliage overhead or from pine branches overhanging a road."[76] The poetic imagery is so engaging, maybe too much, so it has to be carefully contained.

In 1909 Wright discussed ornament for Oak Park's Nineteenth Century Club. He joins in the common critique of "prettifying externals" and argues for ornament being "primarily a spiritual matter...organic with the structure it adorns." He concludes with a striking reversal of previous propositions which may be his effort to address his audience who likely thought ornament was a matter of fashion in clothes and home decoration: "Construction should be decorated. Decoration should be purposely constructed…"[77]

The key to understanding Wright's complex relation to the category of ornament is his relation to Louis Sullivan. Finally, when he was entering his eighth decade and the publication of *Genius and the Mobocracy* (1949), he found a way to focus what ornament meant to him. Its meaning lay in the example of Sullivan's ornament, not for its formal, conventionally familiar aspect, which Wright understood without effort, but for what Wright's power of interpretation abstracted from the examples drawn by Sullivan. The significance of ornament for Wright was something beyond the delight he took in making it in all the media he reveled in. The imagination poured into graphics, glass, terra cotta, fabrics, wood, is stunning. The point here is not to take anything away from that amazing formal activity; he obviously loved it. His understanding of how ornament impacted the experience of his buildings is clear when he writes: "In the openings of my buildings, the glass plays the effect the jewel plays in the category of materials, The element of pattern…may be calculated with reference to the scale of the interior and the scheme of decoration given by, or kept by, the motif of the glass pattern."[78] But when it came to thinking about ornament, what it meant, how its practice could inform architecture, Wright was heading down a completely different road, one that led to almost certain misunderstanding by those lost in convention.

In 1924 commenting on Sullivan's death, Wright gingerly nodded in the direction of what Sullivan's ornament meant to him when he wrote, "Later when I have more in perspective, I intend to write about and illustrate his work. It is too soon now. [Wright was 57.] I hope to make clear in unmistakable concrete terms, what is now necessarily abstract."[79] In that same year he refers to the Auditorium "with its plastic ornamentation."[80] That word "plastic" is one of the ways to understand the kind of abstraction on which he is basing his understanding of ornament's potential. He was reflecting on the sequence he saw in Sullivan's compositions and how it led to his surprising interpretation: "I have drawings in my possession showing the gradual development of Sullivanian ornament from Beaux Arts days and John Edelmann's influence down to the time I, myself drew for him, and unfoldment of the style is unbroken and consistent."[81] When Wright passes close to this subject, one again gets the impression there is a lot left unsaid, and maybe not yet fully understood even by Wright himself.

In 1928, four years after Sullivan's passing, Wright again took up Sullivan's achievement in his fifth essay in the series, "In the Cause of Architecture: The Meaning of Materials—the Kiln," writing, "Louis Sullivan's exuberant, sensuous and brilliant imagination took terra-cotta, and it lived....Into the living intricacy of his loving modulation of surface, 'background'—the curse of all staged ornament—ceased to exist....By way of terra-cotta we have here arrived at the matter of Ornament."[82] The lack of background, the consequence of the "plasticity," one of the two characteristics of the ornament Wright extended to a building as a whole, the other being "continuity," moved the category of ornament to Ornament. The capitalization signals a wholly different category. What that constituted was yet to be determined. He said so explicitly: "As we intend to discuss ornament by itself on its merits later, let us say now that true ornament is of the things, never on it. The Material develops into its own ornamentation by will of the master. He does not impose forms upon it. He develops it into forms from the within which is characteristic of its nature if he is 'the master.'"[83] We have Wright's words as evidence of a complicated process of trying, first to determine, and then to communicate what ornament could mean.

When Wright is presenting a comprehensive overview of his work, as in the 1908 "In the Cause of Architecture" essay and the 1910

Wasmuth portfolio introduction, he feels a necessity to at least refer to ornament in his architecture. In 1930 he presented another overview in the Kahn Lectures at Princeton. As a man in his sixties, and during a period of reduced architectural work that he filled with major writing projects published in 1932, these lectures instigated a look back at this career and a review of what he had accomplished.

In these 1930 lectures, Wright showed design examples. The context of architecture in 1930 was heavily conditioned by "modern architecture." The relation between Wright's designs twenty years before and the response by European architecture concerned him in part because he thought he had already made a modern architecture. The European architects avoided the comprehensive revaluation Wright thought he had begun. They also stressed aspects that sought to erase or overturn the conventions of architecture with a revolutionary excision. That misunderstanding from Wright's point of view was maybe "omissions but evasions. First among these probable evasions is the nature of materials; second is that characteristic architectural element, the third dimension, and third, there is integral ornament. This neglected trinity, it seems to me, constitutes the beating heart of the whole matter of architecture so far as art is concerned."[84] This introductory summation of what Wright was working toward as contrast to contemporary modern architecture is very clear. Materials seemed to take second place in buildings that aspired to a pure abstraction of form sometimes guided by a machine aesthetic. Machines are not stone, or terra cotta and in modern terms, not wood. The third dimension is addressed elsewhere in this review but is illustrated by a specific example of the relation of the wall to the underside of the overhanging roof: "…a plain screen band around the second story above the windowsills, turned up over onto the ceiling beneath the eaves. This screen band was of the same material as the underside of the eaves themselves, or what architects call the 'soffit.'"[85] This fold from wall to roof is a key element in Wright's exploration of the third dimension. He described the same folding of planes on the interior: "Having got what windows and doors there were left lined up and lowered to convenient human height, the ceilings of the rooms, too, could be brought over onto the walls by way of the horizontal, broad bands of plaster on the walls above the windows, the plaster color the same as the room ceilings.... The sense of the whole was broadened and made plastic, too, by this expedient. The enclosing walls and ceilings were thus made to flow together."[86] It is significant that he uses the word *plastic* to describe the point of this formal move. This word signals the connection to what Wright said he learned from Sullivan's ornament. This connection is the key to understanding the significance of "ornament" as a lesson for designing a whole building. Bending around corners, whether wall to wall or ceiling to wall, has formal as well as structural functions that repositioned ornamental patterns. In the amazing murals for the Tavern Room at Midway Gardens, the geometric patterns extend beyond the architectural frame by bending around the corners that would seem to be there to contain them. The mural patterns override the architecture. How could that not be an obvious crossing of proper boundaries? The flat ornament joins the three-dimensional world of architecture like an escaped exotic species.

In the very next paragraph, the content of this conception of ornament is made clear as Wright describes the design of his Prairie houses: "But the 'trim' finally became only a single, flat, narrow horizontal wood band running around the room....The trim merely completed the window and door openings in this same plastic sense. When the interior had thus become wholly plastic, instead of structural, a new element, as I have said, entered architecture. Not alone in the trim, but in numerous ways too tedious to describe in words, this revolutionary sense of the plastic whole, an instinct with me at first, began to work, more and more intelligently and have fascinating unforeseen consequences."[87] By putting "trim" in quotation marks, Wright indicates that he is extracting the work from the conventional context and asking us to see it differently. Further, his reluctance to embark on describing exactly how the reinterpretation results in a new architecture, particularly in distinction to "structural," reveals how carefully he is presenting his goals. This distinction regarding structure had already appeared in the 1901 "Art and Craft" lecture. He makes it clear that buildings put together piece by piece inhibit the creation of architecture as continuity or plasticity. His descriptions of these interiors show how he was trying to make those concepts real even if only indicated by wood strips and plaster. Only later does this "ornamental" technique reach the status of a new way to think about structure. From the graphic indications of plasticity and continuity used in traditional constructional assemblies, Wright immediately embraced reinforced concrete for its seamless embodiment of his abstract, aesthetic goals. Construction with wooden boards and masonry units all reveal the process of assembly; poured concrete does not. This new construction material displaced his inspired, if provisional, use of wood as planar structure tied together with nails and screws. Concrete achieved continuity all at once.

The evident change in Wright's architecture in the latter decades when he embraced reinforced concrete indicates the impact of actually being able to build continuity, not suggest or approximate it. This apparent achievement of his "aesthetic goals" gave up something incorporated in the earlier, partial, means of achieving them. I would identify this characteristic of the earlier work as "legibility." When the means to achieve plasticity and continuity require bringing together pieces to assemble continuity, you could see what was being aimed at and the degree to which it was being accomplished. When the traces of that assemblage were erased, the building was rendered inarticulate, even mute. Reinforced concrete seemed to be the end, the ultimate arrival at the aesthetic goal of continuity overcoming the goal of plasticity. Arrival at such a conclusion may be satisfying but may also be self-defeating because the material struggle is obscured. It becomes gestural rather than communicative. Evidence of the means: tools, the hand, and even machines are missing. The struggle to build is erased in the finished building. During construction of reinforced concrete, of course, there is considerable piecing together in setting up the formwork. One wonders if emphasizing that process by retaining and even featuring the imprint of formwork was a way some architects reminded us how the continuity of concrete was achieved. (Le Corbusier's and Paul Rudolph's concrete come to mind.) The nature of that material resided in how it was handled, not anything inherent in its materiality. By removing any evidence of how it was handled, the abstract goal of continuity was all that remained. The featureless character of Wright's later concrete, smooth like refrigerator cookie dough one observer noted, contributes to the dismissal of what it takes to actually make a building approach plasticity and continuity. One could go so far as to say that in the later years Wright was aiming, or being urged to aim, for an architecture that transcended mere earthly materials. The idea of putting gold leaf on the concrete of Fallingwater is clearly an attempt to shed structure of weight so it floats rather than cantilevers. The reflectivity of gold leaf, inevitably mottled over time, obscures the solidity of the structural members. In that way the building does not correlate with the cantilevered rock ledges under the house but transcends them. Wright's concrete becomes dematerialized structure as his commitment to "spirit" leaves the "nature of materials" far behind. Another example of Wright carrying a metaphor beyond its capacity could be the weaving metaphor pushed to failure in the textile block constructions in California. Those buildings embody the process but ultimately fail as actual constructions.

When he gets to Arizona in 1928–29, he sees "integral ornament in everything." It is found in all kinds of natural phenomena. The desert plants are lessons in structure and ornament. "Nature never sticks ornament onto anything. She gets it all out from the inside of the thing the way it grows."[88] A wonderful unconscious parallel occurs when he cites the "dotted line" as particularly characteristic of the desert plants and then attaches cubes of wood along a soffit resonating with Greek dentils. Here is another crossing over, this time from nature to history.

The Natural House, published in 1954 when Wright was 87, is notable for its more detailed descriptions of what his architecture was like as a material artifact rather than an abstract presentation of "principle." In the opening chapter of *The Natural House*, he clearly separates "ornament" into two categories. In the conventional role of small-scale formal expression, "A new ideal of ornamentation had by now arrived that wiped out all ornament unless it, too, was an integral feature of the whole. True ornament became more desirable than ever but it had to 'mean something'; in other words *be* something organic in character."[89] This ornament is distinct from ornament as a lesson provided by his abstract interpretation of Sullivan. Plasticity is called out in a sub-section to repeat just what he had come to understand about the lessons he learned from Sullivan as he had referred to in *Genius and the Mobocracy* five years before. The "cut-and-butt joinery" is overcome by plasticity achieved by the "expressive flow of continuous surface." The resulting "continuity" approaches the ways botanical nature grows: "as plant grows up out of soil." These two terms learned from Sullivan's ornament are now the "structure of the building itself." "Why a principle working in the part if not living in the whole?"[90]

When Wright goes on to say what the consequences of plasticity and continuity are for architecture, he describes it as: "walls, ceilings, floors...*seen* as component parts of each other, their surfaces flowing into each other...eliminating all constructed feature."[91] He extends this ideal to structure, arguing that when following that goal, plasticity escaped the conventional engineering calculations of the day. When surfaces are seen as continuous by means of the fold that he described earlier at the juncture of ceiling and wall inside and wall and soffit outside, the parts, although joined, do not disappear into a flowing surface. If the parts are like the whole, are they still parts? Where is the "individual" if completely merged into the group?

Continuity is given its own subdivision: "Another Reality: Continuity." The structural manifestation of "the principle of continuity...

[is] called tenuity."[92] Plaited steel strands flow from column to beam, from floor to wall. "Steel in tension enables the support to slide into the supported, or the supported to grow into the support somewhat as a tree-branch glides out of its tree trunk."[93]

Ornament is also given its own category: "Integral Ornament at Last!" What follows is more or less a repeat of what Wright wrote in the Kahn Lectures twenty-five years previously. "Integral ornament is simply structure-pattern made visibly articulate...."[94] The modernist "Ornaphobia" is preferable to "Ornamentia," using Wright's colorful vocabulary. No ornament is better than applied ornament.

Later writings like *A Testament* contain restatements of earlier comments on integral ornament, Sullivan, and poetry of pattern. The work of interpretation of the potential of ornament to inform architecture as a whole has been done. But the lesson is now so integral with the design process it requires no emphasis.

With respect to Gothic cathedrals, the very thing that John Ruskin disliked about the building was how it looked like a ship building site beached on a hilltop. The flying buttresses are a kind of permanent formwork necessary to support the interior vessel. The legibility of the Gothic cathedral was of constructional, structural processes, not the culturally inscribed signs: the pilasters, moldings, cornices one came to read on Renaissance architecture. Wright dismissed that architecture as being blocks carved with signs quoted from historical precedents. The ability to read those signs was possessed by a privileged, educated class of scholars who were the first to write books about architecture by making use of the new technology of the printing press. For all his stone cutting apprenticeship, Palladio, whose illustrated *Four Books on Architecture* (1570), were among the first to be printed, was happy to be renamed with a classical reference and to be included in Gian Giorgio Trissino's circle of cultured patrons. Knowing how to build only served as the material basis for recognition by clients who read and wrote. Wright's prejudice of that kind of learning most likely stemmed from his uncredentialed roots, which he cunningly cultivated even as he sought to overcome them.

The early means Wright used to indicate and then assemble the qualities of plasticity and continuity, particularly in the Oak Park Studio years, are the wood strips he used to connect the planes of plaster in ceilings, walls, and exterior surfaces. Thomas Beeby, Chicago architect and former dean of architecture at Yale, in his important essay "The Grammar of Ornament/Ornament as Grammar," considers the importance of this linear ornament: "Wright had accomplished the task he had set himself; he had evolved a three-dimensional architectural system that achieved what Sullivan had mastered in his ornament."[95] "In a building such as the Unity Temple of 1906, Wright reached a total synthesis of ornament and structure....The structure is designed so as to have an ornamental quality, an example of 'structure ornamentalized'; (from Robert Kerr's lecture to the Royal Institute of British Architects in January of 1869).... This building more than any other is the exact equivalent, in three dimensions, of Sullivan's ornament."[96] Beeby ingeniously describes how analogous Plate 4 in Sullivan's *A System of Architectural Ornament* is to the design of Unity Temple. Taken, not as a stage in a development, but as an achievement, Beeby does not follow out the implications of the sequence of the three stages of the Temple's interior as described in the Introduction of this work. Those implications of a continuity of space and structure represented in the folding of the surfaces indicated by the wooden trim—"It is easy to see [continuity] in the 'folded plane'"— are the primary indicators of Wright's new architecture.[97]

The January 1938 *Architectural Forum* virtually handed over the content and design to Wright to present his recent work in a comprehensive manner. Again there was no direct addressing of the category of ornament. The only compositional example was his citation of the "1-2 triangle," the 30/60 triangle, a common tool on the drafting table. He had introduced this in the Ocatillo desert camp in 1928 as both a section and plan device.

The addition of this angle expanded beyond the orthogonal geometry he had been using from the earliest days. Now "because in itself it has a flexibility in arrangement for human movement not afforded by the rectangle." In discussing the Hanna House (1936), the first extensive use of the 30/60 triangle in plan, he wrote: "The obtuse angle is more suited to human 'to-and-fro' than the right angle. The flow and movement is, in this design, a characteristic lending itself admirable to life, as life is to be lived in it."[98] This interpretation of a geometric figure having significance for human movement is just one more obvious example of how Wright moved from form to function. With the significance of the geometric patterns initiated in ornament, it is unnecessary to decide or recover whether the geometry came before the application to human movement. The reciprocal crossing over from one to the other is the point. That is how Wright stated that form and function are one.

In his writings from the 1930s on, Wright emphasizes "integral ornament" as a new definition of ornament in its more conventional sense. He is making a significant distinction regarding this ornament's sources and contribution to architecture. In discussing the textile block construction in *An Autobiography*, he sums it up: "Here ornament would become a legitimate feature of construction."[99] It is still being referred to as a formal pattern of a certain small scale. There is a section heading, "Integral Ornament at Last," where it is identified with poetry, but more importantly: "Heretofore, I have used the word 'pattern' instead of the word ornament to avoid confusion or to escape the passing prejudice."[100] This statement is clear evidence of how gingerly he approached the category. Now, in his sixties, he is able to go further and say: "Ornament meaning not only surface *qualified by human imagination* but imagination giving *natural pattern* to structure...*itself*."[101] It could not be clearer how pattern, form, is a generator of meaning when he contrasts that source of meaning with "the scholarly architect. A man of taste [becoming] content with symbols."[102]

Although not explicitly referring to ornament, his 1945 "Taliesin Square Paper Number 9" reinforces the larger significance of ornament as lessons for architecture: "...the creative mind sees the basic patterns of construction in the FORM of whatever is. There, within, lie the patterns of being which he sees by abstraction. And such abstractions are architecture."[103] In a nutshell he identifies the basis for his architecture and by implication points out how ornament, which is precipitated FORM, in the broader sense, is the root of architecture.

To return briefly to Semper, his recognition of how buildings differed geographically and materially points out an important emphasis in Wright's work. Semper described the general division of these motives into two fundamental dwelling types: the wall-dominated, or courtyard style, of the south and the roof-dominated, enclosed dwellings of the north. It is clear that the cantilever appears only in the roof world of the north. The direct bearing of wall structure, certainly in masonry as well as post-and-beam construction, does not lead to cantilevers. And before reinforced concrete, cantilevering required linear members usually of wood to deflect the environmental impacts of sun and rain by means of the roof. The architecture of masonry units achieved a single structural unit, the mass element of the wall. Linear constructional elements, historically wood, when assembled, create a readable diagram of design and construction. It is like a steam engine whose parts are visible and invite reading how it works as opposed to an electromotive diesel whose workings are covered by the metal "shroud" that reveals nothing. The linear, diagrammatic method is readable, the mass method is not. The unique property of the Gothic is the unlikely and ultimately unstable transformation of masonry into a linear, geometric network. I think that is exactly why Wright found some sympathy with the Gothic. His proposal for a new architecture left behind the members, the joints, the assembly of parts and sought a continuity that was pointedly different from the masonry blocks of earlier architecture. Articulation of assembled parts would be displaced by continuity. What those abstract goals actually consisted of is worth considering. Were continuity and plasticity achieved by literal surfaces or were they indicated by a mesh of geometry threaded through everything? That distinction may be used to characterize Wright's Prairie work. In the later work, wood was replaced by reinforced concrete that actually constructed abstract aesthetic goals. Wright's use of planar assembly of wooden members as in the Usonian solid wall lamination, his immediate embrace of the new plywood material, are an interim stage of trying to build his aesthetic ideal that he achieved when he turned to concrete.

Ornament that indicated continuity and plasticity because it is composed of large- and small-scale elements seems to disappear when indication is displaced by actual material continuity. Is ornament a booster rocket whose function drops away as articulation is overcome? Transcendence leaves a world of distinction, of parts present in the nature of materials, behind. The counter force to this conclusion is found in Wright's love of pattern. Pattern is not featureless smoothness. Materials other than concrete have patterns that Wright reveled in. So the lessons to be gained from ornament lead to continuity in a literal sense and plasticity that leads to pattern and difference. After a blank sheet is inscribed with a grid, which is a continuous pattern, it is "qualified," a favorite word for Wright, by adding lines that mark wide and narrow zones as in the "tartan grid," the surface acquires a pattern of differences. Adding more and more lines creating tighter and tighter patterns finally results in a black sheet of continuity. The stages of patterns between the two continuities, white and black, are where continuity and plastic differentiation are played out. Wright recrosses the boundary that separates these two goals whenever one asserts priority over the other.

In the Kahn Lectures of 1930, Wright cites the event that confirmed how he got from ornament to structure: "And as further sequence of this idea that plasticity should be at work as continuity in actual construction, from laboratory experiments made at Princeton by Professor Beggs, it appears that the principle of continuity actually worked in physical structure as specific proof of the soundness of the aesthetic ideal."[104]

Wright thought in form first, which was then corroborated as structure by engineers. His understanding of the potentials of form, the "aesthetic ideal," identified by "plasticity" and "continuity" learned from Sullivan, was confirmed by an engineer's analysis of structure. One of the consequences of plasticity and continuity for structural analysis is the complex calculations introduced by indeterminate structures in the early part of the century. Professor of civil engineering for twenty-five years, George E. Beggs (1883–1939), from frustration with the elaborate calculations being used to deal with indeterminate structures, developed a physical modeling technique. (Indeterminate structures are statically indeterminate when the static equilibrium equations—force and moment equilibrium conditions—are insufficient for determining the internal forces and reactions on that structure.) In a paper Beggs delivered in March 1927, he said, "Further knowledge of the action of indeterminate structures will be extended primarily by observation and experiment."[105] By building "models of celluloid or fine quality cardboard...that were not necessarily a small-scale reproduction of the actual structure, but its members are given the same proportion of stiffness as those in the actual structure," direct measurement by micrometers and microscopes of deflections on the models were possible.[106] Dr. Beggs assures that "[t]he accuracy of analysis by elastic models is very satisfactory, as has been proved repeatedly by experiment and by calculation."[107] That technique of direct observation of a model clearly would hold the interest of someone like Wright, whose sense of mathematics was focused on visible mathematics of geometry rather than numerical calculation. How he came to know of Beggs's work is an open question. Maybe he learned of it immediately before he delivered his lectures at Princeton, "From some laboratory experiment at Princeton by Professor Beggs which I saw while there delivering the Kahn Lectures in 1930."[108]

The encounter with the engineer's work clearly indicates that Wright began with a predilection and fascination with form which he then he pursued for its further implications for architecture. Or rather, the two processes were pursued in rapid alternation, crossing back and forth, if you will. In 1927 he had combined the Sullivan concept of plastic with structure crossing over from one to the other: "The design may emphasize the plastic as structural or the structural as plastic."[109] With the citation of the Princeton professor, made when Wright was in his sixties, he finally was able or willing to say how his mind worked. He was fascinated with the manipulation of form particularly in the early decades of his career. Once he had come to some understanding of the larger lessons form could provide, it was still a delight, but the discovery of its larger potentials may have already occurred.

The reluctance to say how he worked may be based in his understanding of how ornament, or form, was considered an insubstantial basis for architecture. For him, form was not an end in itself but it always stimulated sensory satisfaction. His interpretive prowess saw through the satisfaction with form but did not discard it. That is the key, seeing through: "through" is both *beyond* and *by means of*. Form's potential for interpretation beyond its sensory impact is what he sought to base his architecture on. He did not begin with verbal explanations, however much he wrote and said while apparently trying to figure out his intuition and to avoid being misunderstood. He began with his T-square and triangle. Clearly his mind was busy analyzing the activity of his eyes and hands at work. (This could also be an origin of his educational proposition of "Learning by Doing.") It is almost as if he was simultaneously working the drafting tools and looking for its extra-sensory significance.

Explorations of geometry constructed with those tools created a means to consider how things go together; how continuity and plasticity organize many more things than the composition of ornament. He was seeing in Sullivan's ornament implications for thinking about all aspects of architecture. He began wanting to establish the significance of architecture, crossed over into the world of ornament, and then crossed back, having discovered a way to enact function, structure, human life in architectural form. Finding corroboration with his aesthetic goals in the structural analysis by an engineer was the clearest proof of this process. In his commitment to form could be found a whole world of architectural potential. As he put it in *An Autobiography*, published after the Princeton lectures: "But here now ornament is in its place. Ornament meaning not only *surface qualified by human imagination* but...*imagination giving natural pattern to structure itself.*"[110] Finally he is able to summarize how ornament leads to architecture.

Ornament's plasticity and continuity may also provide an explanation why Wright did not top off his pre-war Usonian houses with the more familiar and serviceable hipped roofs. Formal continuity and plastic projection required parallel planes of flat roofs, or maybe it was just his response to the Museum of Modern Art's 1932 exhibition of International Architecture. Of course, his response was not just reaction; he was incorporating a stimulus, as he always did, into his own evolution of ornament leading to architecture.

Reviewing how Wright traversed the various boundaries surrounding ornament points out how all his recursions contributed to an understanding of how architecture could be made. Henri van de Velde, the Dutch architect who was part of the contemporary discussion of ornament's potential and was aware of Frank Lloyd Wright's work, saw how Wright's geometry could be the bridge between two and three dimensions. "He strove for dynamic linear ornament to gradually make its way into the third dimension. In this way, the conceived ornament was transformed into a linear spatial continuum."[111]

The three-step sequence described in the Introduction for the design of the interior ornament of Unity Temple that culminated in this "linear spatial continuum" paralleled the three-step sequence of the construction materials that began with brick and stone and concluded with the continuity of a less costly material, concrete. Not missing a beat, Wright finally accepted concrete and embraced this fortuitous continuity as his contribution to modern architecture. In this "first modern building," he had been led away from traditional construction to discover a new synthesis based on the continuity of material and form.

Although there was a wide range of interpretations of ornament's place in architecture around the turn of the 20th century, evidence of how controversial and ultimately significant it was, Frank Lloyd Wright, standing on Louis Sullivan's shoulders, realized a whole new significance for the lessons ornament could teach. That realization is the result of crossing over the boundary that had conventionally separated ornament from architecture. By so doing, Wright could look at each category, not from its own, internal definition, but from the other category's perspective. A new context opened up the potential for architecture to follow ornament's lead, thereby establishing a new relationship of the two. The coherence traditionally found in history and in nature, in precedent and in visible forms, was available in the abstract patterns so powerfully found in ornament when ornament was no longer seen for itself but was understood as having a much more general potential. At the same time, Wright continued to create ornament, particularly in graphic form, with the same delight and inventiveness present at the outset of his architectural career. Theory never displaced that delight.

The way Wright was able to see those potentials was the result of his habit of crossing boundaries to find possibilities and subtleties otherwise obscured by the separations of convention. We will now examine how Wright's way of writing, aggravating as it sometimes is, demonstrates that continuity of crossovers that characterizes his way of doing and thinking about architecture.

CHAPTER THREE

CROSSING BOUNDARIES IN WRIGHT'S WRITINGS

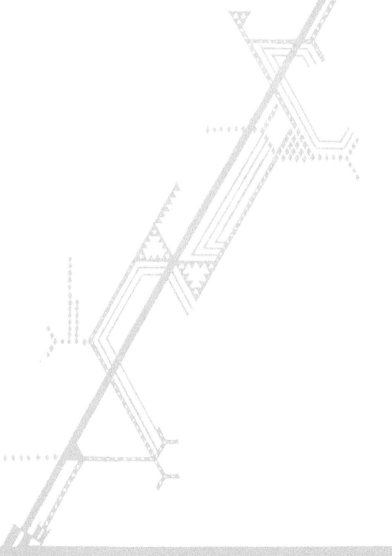

The crossover diagram that motivates this narrative can be applied to Frank Lloyd Wright's composition with words as well as his architecture. Assuming an integral coherence within Wright's activities, a habit of mind, I find he expresses his thoughts on architecture in a pattern parallel with the design of his buildings. He approaches categories of thought—nature, machine, standardization, radical, conservative, organic, to name a few—from one direction and then turns around and looks back to see the category from another side. Whether this move clarifies or confuses, it is likely a rhetorical ploy to avoid being pigeon-holed. But its real significance lies in how it expands categories of thought. Wright's architecture is constructed by walls and volumes that one crosses back and forth, inside and out, room to room, seeing and moving across boundaries going both ways. "Landscape seen through the openings of the building thus placed and proportioned has greater charm than when seen independent of the architecture. Architecture properly studied in relation to the natural features surrounding it is a great clarifier and developer of the beauty of landscape..."[112] "Vista without and vista within."[113] Each is a context for the other. Because figure becomes ground alternatively, nature, for example, is not assigned primacy; it exists in dialog with human purposes.

Rather than being evidence of confusion or inconsistency, Wright's method of exposition, if we are willing to follow it through, demonstrates a way of thinking that shows how categories can reflect on themselves. Simplification is not the goal. This reflexive approach leads Wright to appear to contradict himself. It may challenge easy reading, but it demonstrates complex thinking, which can lead to being misunderstood or, alternatively, to being dismissively understood.

As one example of his categorical intertwining, in 1928 he wraps two conceptions tightly together, one modifying the other in turn.

Beauty always comes to and by means of perfect practicability in architecture. That does not mean that the practicability may not find idealization in realization. On the contrary. Because that is precisely what architecture does and is when it is really architecture. Architecture finds idealization in realization or the reverse if you like.[114]

Realization is made of materials. Idealization is poetry. "The word 'poetry' is a dangerous word to use, and for good reason," Wright observed. "Carl Sandburg once said to me. 'Why do you use the words *poetry, beauty, truth,* or *ideal* anymore? Why don't you just get down to tacks and talk about boards and nails and barn doors?'"[115] Wright understands Sandburg's warning that, when poetry references itself, it is a distraction. For Sandburg poetry is robust only if it rises unbidden from the material specifics. (Emerson made a similar observation about the Transcendentalists: "They have such an image of virtue before their eyes that the poetry of man and nature they never see; the poetry that is man's life…the light that shines on a man's hat, in a child's spoon."[116]) As someone who made material artifacts, Wright knew better than Sandburg. Having poetry in sight conditions the material specifics as much as materials condition poetry. He knew how he idealized and realized together: "To 'idealize' in the fanciful sketch is a thing unknown to me."[117] Sandburg misses how the idealized and the realized are reciprocal. And to be truly poetic does not mean to escape "from life, but does mean life raised to intense significance and higher power."[118] Wright designed an architecture to do just that—for anybody who aspired to such a life for themselves. That aspiration is what democracy allows. Not aspiring is what Wright could not abide.

Wright's apparent reversal of the idealist philosophical sequence of ideal to real is not just contrariness, a charge often made especially when Wright was styled as an impish oracle later in life. How the practical and the beautiful are related has challenged architects forever. When the function of a building changed very slowly, if at all, as in a palace or temple, or most prominently a mausoleum, the beautiful, the non-practical or symbolic was given freer rein to determine the design. Wright's self-proclaimed mission was to make architecture for American democrats, not

European aristocracy who sought to inhabit permanence. To achieve that goal, he showed how the practical and the beautiful ultimately support each other. His restatement of Sullivan's "Form Follows Function" to say, "Form and Function Are One," is further evidence of his project. The way form and function, beauty and practicability, look at each other creates a deep resource for understanding and designing. For Wright, beauty was no longer to be assigned to status or class; for there to be an American architecture it had to be available to anyone. (Not everyone! That is how the hierarchy Wright also believed in could resist a leveling democracy that devolved into what he came to see as the "Mobocracy!") Realizing idealization and idealizing realization works both ways when the architect is at work because design can begin with an idea that then must submit to the world of brick, mortar, wood, glass, etc. At the same time, a material or a process of construction, or a form can generate an idea. When an architect engages the material world, it is not just an individual wrestling with materials as would an artist or sculptor or even a musician. That world includes clients, craftsmen, neighbors, etc., that inspire ideas as well as condition them.

The first paragraph of Wright's 1908 essay, "In the Cause of Architecture," is a primary example of this pattern of complex boundaries in his writing. One can imagine Wright taking particular care with these sentences as they served to introduce his work shown in the subsequent fifty-five pages of photographs to a national audience reading the *Architectural Record*. At age forty he had a lot to show and a lot to say in order to position his work in the discourse of American architecture.

> *Radical though it be, the work here illustrated is dedicated to a cause conservative in the best sense of the word. At no point does it involve denial of the elemental law and order inherent in all great architecture, rather it is a declaration of love for the spirit of that law and order and a reverential recognition of the elements that made its ancient letters in its time vital and beautiful.*[119]

Radical/conservative; denial/declaration; spirit (immaterial)/ elements (material forms); these are pairs of categories Wright sees reflexively, not as opposites. He states and qualifies; he proposes and draws distinctions. Starting off with the word *radical* in a major organ of the American architectural profession is clearly a challenge to readers' expectations. His immediate citation of *conservative* calms potential resistance. He repositions *radical* by correlating it with what is usually considered its opposite. *Conservative* is employed in order to see *radical* in a different light, not opposition but qualification. Immediately, however, *conservative* itself is modified "in the best sense of the word." Ten years later he comes down much harder on the negative aspect of conservatism: "Free to reject what passes for conservative when it is only stupid, or passes for right-mindedness when it is only prejudice."[120] In 1908, *radical* and *conservative* are each cited from within their expected frame of reference and then are seen from outside that frame.

Of course, *radical* is a word Wright used to remind us of its root origin; the root can always be present if it has been conserved. Getting back to an "original" state, erasing misguided compromises that capitulated to evolving conditions, has always been the call of radicals who reject the present state of belief, politics, or artistic practice. Definitions of that original state can be couched as both conservative and radical by showing how each term can be viewed from the perspective of the other. *Conservative* can be a dedication to an original, but it requires there be a recoverable continuity behind the accumulations. *Conservative* also has another meaning that Wright hastened to separate himself from. That meaning preserves the accumulated errors entrenched by habit and enshrined by custom. (In this Wright renewed the late 17th-century literary contest in France between the Ancients and the Moderns who argued whether poets should revere past achievements for having weeded out unsuccessful modes to achieve lasting classical forms, or carry forward the ancients' pursuit of excellence in contemporary circumstances.) A common reading of Wright's first sentence can make "cause conservative" a compound noun: "cause-conservative," rather than "a cause[,] conservative in the best sense of the word." When "dedicated to a cause" is the primary reading, it indicates clearly the motivation to make something better. When "conservative" is read as the introduction to the last phrase, it focuses and modifies just what kind of cause Wright is pursuing.

Wright follows these important introductory sentences with observations that expand their complexity. In the crossover context of *radical* and *conservative*, dedication to the cause is not a denial but a declaration of love. Here Wright is trying to show how he works in the present with awareness of the past. He is not a modern revolutionary, particularly of a European stripe, who finds the past a heavy, distracting burden requiring a scorched-earth campaign. (Or a clever sleight of hand!) For him, an American architect, sympathy with past architecture does not have to be obscured by denigrating or even defacing it with a manifesto of artistic liberation. Of course, he takes every opportunity to castigate the Renaissance ("The Setting Sun All Europe Mistook for Dawn," quoting Victor Hugo). It is not the classical world per se, but its thoughtless mimicking that most upset him. Because that tradition was so egregiously misused, there must have been something lurking in it that made it so easily misappropriated. (One can note that Renaissance architecture was the first "style" to be represented and promoted by the newly invented printing press, i.e., Palladio's 1570 *Four Books on Architecture*. Architecture was no longer a presence but a representation; that was the problem.) Wright states in no uncertain terms that the cause he is dedicated to is radical because it separates the "elements," the specific forms of architecture in the past, from the love for the spirit that lay behind those forms. That spirit is found in the "elemental law and order" that made architecture "vital and beautiful." Wright is not a connoisseur of the artifacts as a historian might be. What he "sees" lies beyond the retina; it is their potential, not their sanctity. On the other hand, he is not dedicated to destroying those ancient examples because their siren call of hallowed convention stifles creativity. He sees *radical* and *conservative* as sharing meanings and potentials for creating great architecture today.

The categories considered here are found in Wright's writings from his early statements in the late 19th century when he was in his thirties up until 1930 when he was in his early sixties. The reason for this limited selection from his writings is based on my estimation that in those early decades he is actively working out how to engage his architecture. Subsequently he is on his way to becoming an oracle. There is a striking change evident in the Kahn Lectures delivered at Princeton in May 1930. In addition to describing how he thinks about architecture, there are extended commentaries on large cultural, social, and urban issues. Bruce Brooks Pfeiffer, the indefatigable collector of Wright's written work in the Rizzoli volumes, makes a significant observation about the changes he sees in the writing style around 1930:

> *Wright's style in writing matured at a slower pace than his style as a builder. In architecture, as he predicted in 1908, his work would "grow more truly simple; more expressive with fewer lines, fewer forms; more articulate with less labor."*
>
> *Eventually the same striving for simplicity would result in his writings. Some of his earlier texts are verbose and difficult to read, sentences roam and are studded with idiosyncratic punctuation.* [121]

Pfeiffer's observations see the change as an advance; I see it as a reduction of intellectual effort. That effort subsides once Wright has reached the heights of self-confidence and pointed aphorisms. The larger issues beyond buildings may have been encouraged by his third and final wife, Olgivanna, whom he married in 1928 and whose interest in spiritual matters left the material world in the shadows. Up to that point, his crossover prose gets to the heart of his struggles to create the architecture he is justly famous for. It is the "complex boundaries" I am positing here that make his buildings and his words so significant. Of course, seeking out statements that support the complex boundary proposition is open to the criticism that one finds what one is looking for. The exercise can descend into stringing a bunch of quotes together. It makes a difference which comes first: the quotes or the string.

It is remarkable that in all of his writings, Wright rarely describes architecture; he is not a docent pointing out what you should see and how you should feel. What he does point out is how to think, how to construct the basis for seeing and designing. We do not go to Wright to read, but to learn to look penetratingly.

MACHINE

When Frank Lloyd Wright writes about the machine, he sees mechanization from the inside out and from the outside in. He responds to its internal potential to contribute to architecture and to its external threat that undermines it. Wright aligns several related categories with the machine; it shares the effects of reduction and simplification with standardization and conventionalization. In turning toward and away from categories like the machine, when he presents the positive functioning of the machine, he immediately tempers that advocacy by its negative impact to avoid being identified as a partisan or more accurately as a one-way thinker. As he stated in the 1930 Kahn Lectures: "Where certain remarks I have made concern nature and romance on one hand, and the machine upon the other, I am accused of inconsistency."[122] Not only is a foolish consistency the hobgoblin of little minds, as Ralph Waldo Emerson pointed out, it suppresses richness of form in architecture and nuance in thought. After all, consistency is simply seeing things from one direction only.

Throughout his career, Wright presents multiple sides of the effect of the machine on architecture. In his "In the Cause of Architecture" (1908), the machine is identified with "cheap repetitions" reproduced "with murderous ubiquity." In contrast, two years later, the essay introducing the German folio of his work *Ausgeführte Bauten und Entwürfe,* finds the machine producing "that simplicity of rendering [which the machine] makes not only imperative but opportune."[123]

Wright sets up his complex relation to the machine in his most important early public presentation, "The Art and Craft of the Machine" lecture he gave in 1901. Promoting the machine to the Arts and Crafts Society in Chicago seems like a challenge, but the role the machine had in contemporary artistic and architectural practice did not require the same defensive posture in Chicago as might be required if addressing readers of John Ruskin or William Morris in England. Wright's title was undoubtedly a challenge, but he explored the relationship of craft and machine by seeing how the machine had both positive and negative consequences. By 1928 he could clearly say that a building is "an entity perfected by the Machine, but not for the Machine, nor as a Machine."[124] Here are three aspects of how the machine and architecture are related. It is a tool in the service of architecture, not architecture in service to mechanical prerequisites, nor architecture effacing itself in servitude to a new spirit of an age dominated by the machine. Wright is clearly resisting fashionable momentum that seeks to displace architecture's historical role by something modern.

The very title "The Art and Craft of the Machine" puts categories conventionally thought of as adversaries in a complementary relation. It was surely Wright's intention to be a challenge, but his examination of their usually contentious relationship demonstrated the way of thinking and designing that was characteristic for the rest of his career. In the 19th century, the machine was posed as the enemy of art and craft by the likes of Ruskin and Morris. To see the machine as contributing to art and craft flew in the face of this received evaluation. Wright breaks down the barriers between the two categories so they can each be understood by crossing over the complex barrier between them. "In the machine lies the only future of art and craft — as I believe, a glorious future....

[T]he machine is, in fact, the metamorphosis of ancient art and craft."[125] In later paragraphs he presents the machine in an unfavorable light: "…it made…a terrible engine of enslavement, deluging the civilized world with a murderous ubiquity…"[126] Wright can say both apparently contradictory things by positing an internal distinction within the category of "art." Art was both a boneyard of past forms, and the eternal expression of the spirit of law and order underlying its continuing vital present. So the machine interacted with art "in the old" sense very differently from its contribution to the spirit of art in the present.

In a stunning correlation, he conflates the machine with the printing press to create a further example of something as both threat and opportunity. Quoting Victor Hugo's *Notre Dame de Paris* chapter "Ceci Tuera Cela," ("This Will Kill That" or, as Wright clarifies it, "The Book Will Kill the Edifice"), Wright identifies the mechanical reproduction of the poet's work as "perpetuating [human thought] more resisting than architecture…more simple and easy."[127] "Printed, thought is more imperishable than ever—it is volatile, indestructible. As architecture[,] [thought] was solid; it is now alive; it passes from duration in point of time to immortality."[128] "Probably Gutenberg's invention of movable types was the first great advent of the machine in any sweeping form. The blessing of that invention is obvious as is the curse that came with it."[129]

For an architect to admit the endurance of printed words reproduced by the machine is greater than the singular material endurance of a building is a serious observation. One might imagine that this implied threat to the great art whose decaying remnants stand for the record of civilization motivated Wright to find a way to maintain architecture's preeminent status. Rather than the unique edifice, the machine could produce models of architecture for anyone, i.e. the private house, continuously constructed for evolving generations. If the printing press gave individuals their own copy of the poet's verses, the machine could give individuals their own example of architecture to inhabit, not as a commodity but as art. Whether his American System-Built examples were commodity or art describes the complex boundary separating these two categories.

Wright lamented that his Lieber Meister Louis Sullivan ended his career by retreating into the book. When he writes, "[Sullivan] was compelled to win recognition in a medium that is the all-devouring monster of the age," he calls that medium "the literal art." It is one of the "great Arts," so he must mean literature, but it has "sapped the life and strength… to the everlasting harm of culture and good life." "Inasmuch as there are five senses, five avenues open to man's communion with Life—four-fifths of human sensibility is lost when one Art usurps the place of the other four. Human beings are fast becoming human documents…"[130] Of course, Wright himself willingly worked in the realm of words spoken and printed.

"The machine is capable of carrying to fruition high ideals in art—higher than world has yet seen!"[131] He even finds an "organic nature of the machine," as he praises "the universal automatic fabric: the engine, the motor, and the battleship, works of art of the century!"[132] Later he expands this striking correlation: "Therefore, of the essence of this thing we call the Machine, which is no more or less than the principle of organic growth working irresistibly the Will of Life though the medium of Man."[133] It seems Wright is crisscrossing borders of categories and evaluations uncontrollably. On the face of it, the last thing a machine would seem to be is "organic." But, of course, it is not the machine itself that can be so described. Instead *organic* describes an evolution of its role as yet another tool in the hand of an artist that extends the means to realize "that law and order" in its time.

Wright ascribes several roles to the word *machine*. The destructive power of the machine can be seen in "man's early art idealized, now reduced to its lowest terms…swiftly and surely destroying itself through the medium of the Machine."[134] Misunderstanding the machine as an independent force, not a means to extend artistic evolution, institutes its negative capacity. Going further, Wright asserts, "Machinery has been invented for no other purpose than to imitate…"[135] In a powerful conclusion to the 1901 lecture, Wright pauses to observe: "Now, let us ask ourselves whether the fear of the higher artistic expression demanded by the Machine, so thoroughly grounded in the arts and crafts, is founded upon a finely guarded reticence, a recognition of inherent weakness or plain ignorance."[136] To propose "higher artistic expression demanded by the Machine" is a bold statement cutting through all the accumulated, 19th-century resistance to the degrading impact of the machine on art and craft. It takes strength and fortitude to stare the machine in the face, look aside from its destructive activity, and see that the conflict between art, craft, and the machine is the consequence, not only of weakness, but of the perpetuation of categories instead of processes.

In 1924, when writing shortly after Louis Sullivan's death, Wright saw machine's negative aspect from the perspective of Sullivan's declining career: "Machine-made life in a Machine-age that steadily automatizes, standardizes, amortizes the loving beauty of Life he knew and loved and served so well — seems desolation, damnation!"[137] This context is less about architecture and more about society, culture, the misdirected evolution that took a different tack than the one Wright hoped for twenty-three years before. Wright at thirty-four had seen a different world with different eyes than a man fifty-six years old at an uncertain point in his career. (Nineteen-thirty was not a time of active commissions, or the promise of them, for Wright.)

The machine is reviewed positively in the next year as Wright returns to the making of buildings that his "In the Cause of Architecture" essay announced as the "Third Dimension." He returns to the observations made in the 1901 talk to see the machine as having a salutary impact on the way materials are understood free from the craftsman's hand. "In all the crafts, the nature of materials is emancipated by the machine, and the artist is free from bondage to the old post-and-lintel form, the pilaster and architrave are senseless, and Architecture in superimposed layers is now an 'imposition' in every sense....The principle of the Machine is the very principle of Civilization itself now focused in mechanical forms."[138] This last statement can be read in more than one way; is it positive or not? But a following sentence clarifies that uncertainty: "Standardization and repetition realized and beautified as a service rendered by the machine and not as a curse upon the civilization that is irresistibly committed to it."[139] But again, is irresistible commitment positive or not? The commitment to the machine does not seem like a choice if it is irresistible. Does that make it inevitable? Wright sees art and its tools as proceeding in time in an organic evolution. What is not inevitable is the way tools are used.

The machine opens new ways not only to make art, but to imagine it. "Time was when the hand wrought. Time is here when the *process* fabricates instead."[140] You can see Wright establishing continuity while carefully making distinctions. Like "conservative," the machine "in the best sense of the word" is the next tool that can continue that "spirit of law and order" underlying all great architecture. As a lifter of drudgery from the shoulders of Americans, the machine is "the forerunner of Democracy." And at the same time by "the modern machine we have built up a monster image of ourselves...[that] will eventually destroy us unless we conquer it—and turn it from its work of enslavement to its proper and ordained work of emancipation."[141] Wright draws an unexpected connection between Nature and the Machine: "Therefore build Nature-patterns in terms of such materials as best suit our human-nature, this and our Architecture will be the greater for the Machine."[142] Clearly he discounts the back-wash of machine patterns compromising any activity where it can be employed; he has confidence in the human condition where machines could be used to retain connection to Nature in whatever guise. Or does he? "Architecture expresses human life, machines do not." So where does Wright stand in the subject of the machine? "As for beauty — standardization and its cruel but honest tool, the machine..."[143] He is not deliberately being self-contradictory, a trickster donning a whole collection of masks. His course is not comfortable, reassuring. It is a challenge he sets for himself and he only respects those who take it up for themselves. The goal evident in his way of presenting his thought is to keep moving, over and back, avoiding at all costs getting stuck in one reductive posture or another. The excitement of going in and out of his rooms and buildings parallels the paths taken when following his boundary-crossing thoughts.

STANDARDIZATION

Standardization, one consequence of the machine, like the machine itself, can also be approached from its internal positive potential and its external negative impact. "Standardization as a principle is the most basic element in civilization. To a degree it is civilization itself."[144] This and the following observations appeared in Wright's set of "In the Cause of Architecture" essays published in the *Architectural Record* in the mid-1920s. Of course, Wright crossed over the distinction between standardization and the machine when he also says: "The principle of the Machine is the very principle of civilization itself now focused in mechanical forms."[145] The connection is: "…the Machine [i]s the tool of standardization."[146] This proposition recognizes that patterns—language, symbols, social structures—all contribute to organizing individual lives and experiences, enabling community and making communication possible. When Wright refers to "law and order" in his 1908 essay, it is that spirit that makes architecture possible. However, he goes on to observe: "Standardization can be murderer or beneficent…the thing standardized is kept by imagination or destroyed by the lack of it."[147] He goes further: "Standardization was already inflexible necessity [whether] enemy or friend—you might choose."[148] Wright sets up the choice, the consequences, and calls on you to consider them. Wright's recognition of the complexities bordering any category does not make him an effective advocate of simple proclamation. He does not write effective manifestos, except maybe later when he becomes a disruptive gadfly. To select isolated statements from the first half of his career to make him seem an oracle does a great injustice to the depth of his work.

Monotony, one of the fallouts of the repetitive mechanical process, is the consequence of the lack of imagination. "Standardization apprehended as a principle of order has the danger of monotony in application."[149] When standardization is viewed from the perspective of its capacity to produce simplicity, its reductiveness can lead to principle. "The process of elimination which standardization becomes has left only essentials."[150] The elimination of the circumstantial and the superficial leaves only the core, the essence. When its reductiveness is seen as sameness, standardization is a threat. "So this very useful tendency in the nature of the human mind, to standardize, is something to guard against as thought and feeling are about to take 'form' — something of which to beware — something to be watched…standardization should be allowed to work but never to master the process that yields the forms."[151] The repetition that is at the heart of the machine's operation produces artifacts whose interchangeability eliminates differences separating them from craft production. The unique is suppressed in favor of the conventional.

Standards are the enforcement technique of standardization. Any time Wright encountered standards, he knew he was in the presence of someone or some group seeking to limit or curtail individual initiative. They were a threat to his freedom. Whether it was the AIA — the "Arbitrary Institute of Appearances," as Wright referred to it — or more seriously the academy, standards were what institutions imposed. Standardization is parallel to institutionalization. When the Fellowship was set up at Taliesin in 1932, he would not have tarnished it by calling it a school. After his death that organization countered his suspicion of institutions and transformed into an accredited degree-granting school whose future was irretrievably compromised.

Standardization is one way to describe the "unit system" that Wright initiated in the Oak Park Studio practice in the first decade of the

20th century and beyond. Tasks are often accomplished by the contribution previous experience makes to the present task. A context precedes the task at hand. A skilled worker must balance the unique, immediate task with the foreknowledge brought to it from previous efforts. (This balance is not that remote from the concurrent roles of the individual and the citizen; the citizen is an individual in a context.) He described the positive effect of standardization by means of the craft of weaving when he used the textile metaphor explicitly in the "textile block" houses of the 1920s. The constructional "grid" of the loom pervades Wright's architecture. In contrast, sculptural figures (Greek temples, for example) stand alone as bounded artifacts poised in the landscape. Wright's buildings are purposefully enmeshed in geometry elicited from an abstracted nature similarly patterned.

The textile block houses in California in the 1920s may be a too literal application of a network of geometry attested to by their constructional failures. A web of pattern is always present in Wright's designs, however. The carpets of Persia were examples of the discipline of the warp serving as the base for the color and pattern of the weft. With the unit-system, "a certain *standardization* is established here at the beginning. Like the warp with the oriental rug. It has other and economic values in construction...."[152] In 1908 he introduces the idea with reference to the "warp and woof [weft] of the structure." He described the Imperial Hotel in similar terms: "It is really a gigantic masonry brocade of brick and stone and copper fused together with concrete inlaid with steel fiber."[153] "At intersections of laterals and verticals, the reinforcement was interlocked on the principle of flexibility..."[154] The correlation of discipline, of construction, of principle and the immediate circumstances of imagination, of context, of social setting is the elusive result Wright sought as he uncovered the potentials of form. One could make a parallel that the warp is conservative and the weft is radical. Creating artifacts and propositions that incorporate the best of both qualities is Wright's constant goal.

CONVENTIONALIZATION

If *standardization* is primarily a technical term, *conventionalization* is a cultural term. Frank Lloyd Wright approaches and reconsiders the category of conventionalization, like the category conservative, as both contributing to architecture and constraining it. From one side of the internal boundary within conventionalization, it can have a positive contribution to architecture. Cross over that boundary and it is seen to have negative consequences. When Wright uses the word *conventionalization*, he immediately warns us: "I wish I might use another word..."[155] Just as he qualifies "conservative in the best sense of the word," conventionalization contains a boundary he crosses over to pick up both what it can contribute and what it critiques. For Wright, the categories of the machine and standardization intersected with the broader category of conventionalization because each of them helped to explain how he worked to pare away the circumstantial to arrive at principle, the underlying continuity of law and order, the foundation of great architecture. The simplification achieved by the machine, by standardization, and by conventionalization removes the insignificant and leaves only the significant pattern that underlies the superficial. Although Wright does not go into the connection in the 1927 essay "In the Cause of Architecture: Architecture and the Machine," standardization is at least parallel with one of his cherished categories, conventionalization.

In the positive perspective, conventionalization is the most consequential simplifying category when Wright applies it to nature. The convention he is rejecting makes nature a picturesque artifact, or a world "red in tooth and claw," as Alfred Lord Tennyson wrote in *In Memoriam A.H.H.* in 1850. Conventionalization is a process that precedes those categories. For Wright, the process establishes a base, an underlying structure that supports further construction. Its foundational role sets up a way to understand and make use of natural phenomena by artists and architects. Wright's extension of the process reaches beyond organizing visual structures to organizing the ways people relate to one another. It sets up an underlying structure for community: "…this natural state, conventionalized harmoniously with the life principle of all men."[156] When someone who often extols the value of individual freedom presents this aspect of conventionalization, a boundary has clearly been crossed. Engendering frustration or understanding is what this argument about crossing boundaries is all about. Convention is initially some kind of agreement with other people past or present. It also constrains the individual by aligning it with a community. Aligning with other people is not something Frank Lloyd Wright embraced; they were to align with him. Freedom in this conventionalization is the freedom to pursue principle available to anyone who makes the effort Wright makes.

Wright introduces the category of conventionalization with particular emphasis when presenting his high regard for the Japanese wood-block prints. It may seem unusual for an American architect at the beginning of the 20th century to place such value on the two-dimensional graphic art of an Asian artistic culture. Beginning with his first foray into Japan in 1905 when he was thirty-eight years old, just finishing the groundbreaking Larkin Building, and ready to directly consult a new source for his work, Wright became a recognized connoisseur and collector of the prints. He devoted considerable time and money acquiring the prints, exhibiting them, and writing about their significance to his own work. A concise discussion of the prints is found in his monograph *The Japanese Print* (1912). It summarizes his earlier commentary extolling the prints' virtues. His approach to the prints is not simply that of a collector or a member of the cognoscenti as the subtitle of the title essay — "An Interpretation" — makes clear. The essay explains how the prints inform the work of an architect. After learning about them, studying them, what happens next in Wright's interpretive effort proves their significance. I hasten to add that, in respect of Wright's undeniable creativity, what lies between a Japanese print and a Wright building is a giant black box. No one can seriously say they can draw a line between the two.

The appeal of the graphic patterns and colors on an aesthetic basis certainly initiates Wright's appreciation. Seeing the "subject" simultaneously with the graphic pattern is another instance of seeing circumstantial nature and the abstract order underlying its appearance. The contemporary interest in the prints, the parallels with the graphic patterns of the Art Nouveau (of Brussels, Vienna, and Glasgow), reveal Wright's artistic preferences. Some of the more direct links to the prints appear in the representations of Wright's designs throughout his career, particularly in the plates of the 1910 Wasmuth portfolio. The most often cited example is the dramatic upward-looking perspective of the Hardy House on the shore of Lake Michigan in Racine, Wisconsin. The tall framing with the subject way at the top recalls Japanese scrolls. The framing of foliage merging with the building is further evidence of the appreciation of Japanese graphic art in the Oak Park Studio by Wright and particularly Marion Mahony.

Wright's commentary on the Japanese print has implications with society, technology, and aesthetics. The prints' replicability contributed to Wright's efforts to make art and architecture available to a democratic American culture as distinguished from a tradition of unique masterpieces collected by European aristocracy. Wright sees this graphic art as instructive on two levels. First, it is art that can be distributed to anyone; it is multiple; it is democratic. It is the visual art equivalent of distributing poetry by the printed book. (The printed book that will destroy the aristocratic edifice but enable the democratic domicile.) That did not prevent him from appreciating the stunning screens of Ogata Kōrin, for example. "To conventionalize is, in a sense, to simplify; and so these drawings are all conventional, subtly geometrical, imbued at the same time with symbolic values, thus symbolism honestly built upon a mathematical basis, as the woof of the weave is built upon the warp." "To dramatize is always to conventionalize."[157] Mathematics, symbolism, and drama are subsumed under conventionalization!

Conventionalization provides Wright with a link to his central category, nature, a site where his interpretive crossovers abound. The first contact with nature is the plethora of phenomena that our senses register. In order to survive this experiential overload, we pay attention selectively. We place the immediate stimuli in a context of similar events. This initial move diminishes the specific event's uniqueness in favor of its position in a structure. That structure can be characterized as abstract. In so far as that abstraction separates us from the immediate impact of the unique particulars of sensory experience, it constrains the individuality of that particular experience. "But however much we may love oak or pine in a state of Nature their freedom is not for us. It belongs to us no longer, however much the afterglow of barbarism within us may yearn for it. Real civilization means for us a right conventionalizing of our original state of Nature."[158] Wright recognizes the cost of conventionalization, the placement of the individual in a context that circumscribes its potential, but the reward is the context that links experiences together, structures them to contribute to larger significances.

Taking in and interpreting the stimuli we experience in the natural world is important to Wright. The sequence of the process of imagining, disciplining, designing always starts with sensory experience. It is also the sequence in encountering a work of art. To stop with the retina, to name only one sense, is to build experience on foundations of sand. "All we were given of love for the picturesque in gesture, form, color, or sound—gifts to the five senses—is realized. Appearances are expanded into a synthesis of the five senses—we may call it a sixth if we please — and all become manifest materialization of Spirit."[159] The natural world is not free of human manipulation, but its specifics taken in by the senses constitute a powerful aesthetic component.

My use of the word *component* links this observation with F.S.C. Northrup's proposition that our understanding of the world has two components: theoretical and aesthetic. I was introduced to Northrup's *The*

Meeting of East and West by Bob Warn in a lecture on Frank Lloyd Wright that he gave at Carleton College in 1962. Warn had spent time at Wright's Taliesin Fellowship (1945–1948) and found Northrup's proposition useful for understanding Wright.

Now, of course, any East/West characterization is highly suspect, and I am not following Northrup into that territory. But his structure of the theoretical and the aesthetic provides a way to consider how Wright worked. Northrup (1893–1992) was the Sterling Professor of philosophy and law at Yale, whose philosophy correlated Einstein and Alfred North Whitehead. Northrup uses an example to illustrate his construction of understanding based on two concepts: intuition and postulation. Helen Keller, blind from childhood, could understand the category "blue" as a measurement of light waves, a theoretical construction, but she could not know "blue" as a sensory experience. Frank Lloyd Wright encountered nature using geometry as the abstract theoretical component and the immediate sensory stimulation as an aesthetic component. His approach to nature was not theoretical first, aesthetic next, but alternated in both directions. Conventionalization is itself a construction that directs and is a consequence of the human mind encountering the natural world. That mind has the predilection to organize stimuli into patterns, and once it possesses those patterns, the natural world is seen differently.

Geometry is brought together with a sensory experience as raw materials for Wright's compositions. Geometry serves as the instrument of conventionalization that Wright saw the Japanese print artists use to create their compositions. What could be gained by bringing conventionalization to suppress the rich variation of immediate experience? The answer is an understanding of structure, of pattern that transforms the natural world into useful human creations. Seeing how nature is transformed for use by an architect is central to understanding Wright; he is not looking out the window and simply sketching what he sees.

The Japanese wood-block print artist does not depict a particular pine tree but recognizes that all pine trees share identifiable characteristics. The process of simplification conventionalizes the endless variation of nature by structuring the depiction as part of a geometric pattern. "These problems of right aesthetic conventionalization of natural things, revealing the potential poetry of nature as it may be required to make them live in the arts."[160] Again, there is conventionalization that helps consider the unique and the categorization that suppresses it. The initial delight in the natural world as we experience it is basically consumption. The next thing is to see how that material can be interpreted for further action. It is an active encounter with the natural world. Curating those experiences, savoring them, enjoying them ascribes their significance to their impact on us. That stage prepares Wright to construct the patterns of conventionalization as the primary tool for doing the work of interpretation.

When Louis Sullivan's geometry rises from two dimensions into three, it casts shadows. His drawings of ornament become three-dimensional when he draws the shadows. These shadows enable legibility, and reading them was the task of the skilled craftsmen who rendered them in plaster or metal or, in the case of the Banqueting Hall in the Auditorium Building, in wood. When shadows appear in depictions of a natural scene, they are circumstantial, they purport to present a material place. Their introduction in European painting in the Renaissance and after, particularly in voluptuous 19th-century paintings, dramatizes the immediate. They are the product of the position of the light source, the original source being the sun. That source changes. Shadows implicate time. Conventionalization of natural scenes rejects that goal of illusion in favor of a representation that is free of the variations of light, of time. Shadows, however, can aid in representing the projection and recesses of the third dimension. The Japanese prints have no shadows, their conventionalization is poised abstraction setting aside an illusory immediacy. For Wright that graphic flatness is a lesson in getting beyond the illusion to a version of enduring principle. Wright responded to turn-of-the-century artists like Pierre Puvis de Chavannes and Aubrey Beardsley, who also worked in a poised, shadowless world.

The Japanese wood-block print is poised between two dimensions as a graphic representation and a three-dimensional subject. A less obvious characteristic is its avoidance of shadows. Wright has a couple of observations about shadows that direct attention to their role in his aesthetic. "Shadows have been the brushwork of the architect when he modeled his architectural forms. Let him work, now, with light diffused, light refracted, light reflected, use light for its own sake, shadows aside."[161] The light Wright is recommending is light that suffuses; it does not create pools of inky shadows. Sentimental nature leads to representation through "fleshly shade and materialistic shadow" (Sullivan's soft pencil foliage rendered shadow wrapping geometric armature).[162] Such negative characterization of representational shadows indicates how unique circumstances need to be transformed to be made useful for further aesthetic work. Left in compositions, they are relegated to simple consumption. The role of shadows in Sullivan's drawings of ornament is significant. When he picks up his soft pencil, Sullivan draws shadows. When Wright stops short of that move and stays with the geometric armature that precedes the shadows, he synthetizes the theoretical and aesthetic.

Conventionalization has a profound impact on the third dimension. At the same time Wright repeatedly advocates for the third dimension, how does he represent that in the absence of shadows in his drawings? The masterful collection of the graphic images of his buildings in the Wasmuth folio have a distinctive representation of shadows; a barely visible curtain of parallel lines that do not darken the surface they are drawn on. The third dimension in these perspective renderings of his buildings is readable, but not distracting or obscuring.

Trying to stabilize the waywardness of late 19th-century architectural finery, Wright finds sources that can exert discipline and rule. The principles of classical architecture on the one hand and the conventionalization of the Japanese print on the other are two strikingly remote sources he calls upon to organize his fertile imagination. Their sense of control within a tradition of convention, not their particular means, served Wright well to balance imagination and discipline.

NATURE

Now we come to two of the blurriest categories in Frank Lloyd Wright's lexicon: nature and organic. The blur comes from his rapid proposing and taking exception with the boundaries that convention uses to define them. We will begin with nature. If ever there was a word or category that Wright saw from myriad directions, it is this one. Because it is so varied, this review will only pick up the highlights, the most significant internal crossovers in his use of the word. Some of these aspects of nature have already been addressed above as evidence of the complex boundaries between and, more importantly, within these categories. If the machine, standardization, and conventionalization have direct effects on the design of architecture, nature and organic are much broader and connect way beyond the design of a building. They are not unconnected, just connected to many other things.

Very early this category, nature, was elusive. In 1894, when Wright was 27, he wrote: "Shape [the house] to sympathize with the natural surroundings if Nature is manifest there, and if not, try to be as quiet, substantial, and organic as she would have been if she had the chance."[163] "Quiet, thoughtful consistency brings this harmony" to architecture.[164] This enigmatic proposition contains the kernel of what Wright struggled to say and to build for the next seven decades.

If one cannot respond to nature because it is not "manifest" in the immediate context, where is this quiet consistency to be found? It resides in what the mind of the architect brings to the task. Nature is a category with an internal boundary distinguishing between the immediate sensory experience and the mind that organizes that experience. If the architect cannot find the kind of nature that is needed to contribute to design in the given context, the requirement that architecture be based on that nature must be found elsewhere. So that "quiet, substantial, and organic" quality does not reside exclusively in nature. Nature is not the unique source of that quality. Proposing that the human mind with its fund of previous experience and its habit of abstraction can supply what nature would have provided, removes nature from its primary role. Nature was a source, but only when interpreted by man.

The simplest distinction within the category of nature is what is seen and what is proposed to lie beneath what is seen; nature and the nature of. Such a distinction is hardly unique to Wright. He even cites Plato's proposition that what is elementally reliable is the "form" that lies behind what is seen. Wright's citation is not part of a philosophical discussion, however. It occurs in his appreciation of what he sees as the abstraction underlying the images in Japanese prints.

Wright was not engaged with the philosophical propositions Plato was exploring in the Allegory of the Cave. Plato describes how in order to achieve wisdom, people trapped by their illusions must escape the condition that creates those illusions; how people who from childhood are trapped in a cave, are focused on the back wall of the cave and only see shadows as evidence of the world. Those shadows are projected by the light of a fire hidden by a wall behind them. Actors between the fire and the shielding wall hold up puppets that they manipulate to create the shadows of illusion on the back wall. As Plato points out, both the fire and the puppets are the creations of artists. Neither the light nor the puppets are part of ultimate reality which is accessible only when one escapes the cave into the light of the sun.

The image of that allegory was useful to Wright aside from what Plato was proposing. (A characteristic repurposing rather than understanding.) Wright constructs the distinction of the seen and the unseen so he can use nature as both a principle and as raw material. As he says repeatedly in various forms when he is describing nature: "I do not of course mean that outward aspect which strikes the eye as a visual image...but that inner harmony which penetrates the outward form."[165] That inner harmony whose stillness bespeaks of the eternal is Plato's "eternal idea of the thing." Wright is no Platonist in a philosophical sense. The form behind appearance that is accessible through rational thought is not his goal. He is not looking for a booster rocket to leave the material earth behind. He expresses his deep commitment to form: "Ideas exist for us alone by virtue of form."[166] Wright's form is what is seen; it is not Plato's *noumenon*. Seeing appearances is where Wright begins and ends; he loves the material world; he is not trying to escape it: "...Living on Earth *is* a materialization of spirit instead of trying to make our dwelling here a spiritualization of matter." Maybe Wright really is a Hegelian Idealist! But no, he immediately qualifies, as is his habit of recursive thought: "Idealism and Idealist are the same failure as Realism and Realistic.... Already I have dared enough. Try to see—in work."[167] It is difficult not to see here evidence of the habit of crossing over even in the denial. The material world constructed by the architect is, at once, a conclusion and the beginning of its effect on human life.

What is seen—appearance—takes on a completely new significance when looked at from the other side of the boundary between appearance and underlying, abstract pattern. Immediately sensory stimulus and abstract pattern are seen simultaneously. The unseen world of this abstract principle: "For the laws of the beautiful are immutable as those of elementary physics. Laws pre-exist any perception of them; inhere, latent, and effective, in man's nature and his world."[168] These laws have a crucial impact on how appearances can be understood, and more importantly, how they can be structured for use by the architect. The delight in form conditioned by this new perspective acquires a significance and potential it previously did not possess. "'Nature'...has nothing to do with realistic or realism, but refers to the essential *reality* of things. So far as we may perceive reality." The visible world is "external nature."[169] Its other abstract form is found or produced by the human mind. Citing Plato provides cultural cachet for a substantially self-taught young architect, but Wright uses that vocabulary for his own purposes to assert that he is not just an arranger of forms. He sees form as having significant implications beyond the retina.

Where Plato sees illusion, Wright sees the only access to the abstract armature supporting appearance. While form is the initial experience, it is seen as evidence of another world of stable, timeless abstractions that underly all the circumstantial variations of appearance. "Ideas exist for us alone by virtue of form."[170] The diagram of Plato's allegory of the cave suggests how escaping belief in the illusions of the shadows leads out of the cave into the sunlit realm of rational thought. What is not so clear is what to do with the players and their puppets casting the shadows projected by the fire. Those apparently are material entities, but they preexist the illusions. They could be seen as the patterns that create the world of appearances. They are not the appearances, but they project them. They have a status above those appearances, but they are still in the cave. Turning around reveals their underlying source of the appearances. The boundary separating the shadows from the players is crossed over by turning toward and away alternatively. In a literal reading of the allegory, it means looking at the puppeteers and their puppets whose profiles are seen on the wall as the source for the shadows. Wright is not interested in turning away from the illusions of the shadows in order to leave the cave completely, as the Platonic philosopher does.

The means to access the reality, the form behind the visible form, is geometry. The implication is that what is seen as nature is in reality a set of stimuli arrayed on an armature of geometric patterns, a fabric of pattern underlying everything we see. "There is a life-principle expressed in geometry at the center of every Nature-form we see. This integral pattern is abstract, lying within the object we see and that we recognize as concrete form. This hidden form-world is inherent in all forms. This form world is the architect's world. His thought must penetrate that world.... [T]he mind of the artist was touched by that form whatever it might be.... Realism, now is as dead as realistic."[171]

This distinction is clear and constant in Wright's comments on nature. Nature was out there and in here, in the human mind. Wright is not "obedient," he is an active interpreter turning it to his own purposes. Nature is also what is characteristic of a thing itself: human nature, nature of materials, etc. Wright acknowledges the conventional enjoyment of nature: "...[T]he innocent and vivid joy...is yours in the flower of the field and garden."[172] Those sensuous qualities strike a "sympathetic chord in us." The sentiment aroused by this nature cannot be denied, particularly when "to know a thing...a man must first love the thing."[173] But this attraction and delight, once enjoyed, must lead to aesthetic abstractions based in geometry if nature is to be a source for design. "A splendid enrichment of life. The Pictorial is merely an incident and an aim...no longer an end sought for its own sake...NATURE gradually apprehended as the principle of Life—the life-giving principle in making things with the mind..."[174] In a letter from 1897, French Post-Impressionist painter Paul Cezanne (1839–1906) distilled what is also Wright's relation to nature by saying: "Art is a harmony parallel to nature." This brief sentence contains the whole matter: there is nature, the world we are in that we did not make; there is harmony which is a quality humans strive to create and to find in nature or project onto it; and there is a human activity, art, that is not nature but parallels the harmony to be found there. From this perspective, there is no inherent hierarchy of significance when considering art and nature; they each interact across the line that human consciousness defines as the difference between the products of nature and the artifacts of human creation.[175]

To move beyond the sensory consumption of nature, to make it useful, nature needed to be disciplined by a structure underneath the surface delights. Geometry is a curious phenomenon: is it "discovered" or created by the human mind? It seems more foundational and eternal than historical or cultural change would suggest. A circle is the same for an architect of the Third Dynasty in Egypt, of medieval Europe, or 20th-century Japan.

That enigmatic statement of 1894, "The Architect and the Machine," cites what qualities nature supplies to an architect: quiet, substance, organic.[176] An interesting list; quiet, repose, sense of completion, all appear in Wright's description of the desired condition of architecture before he is thirty. To think of nature in these terms is certainly selective. Wright's nature is apparently some remove from the world of donkeys, or people, for that matter. Wright goes to a version of nature whose form can be abstracted with geometry so it can suggest how a building could be designed. It is trees, flowers, and crystals, although the latter tend to be less subject to the changes wrought by the passage of time (i.e., crystals are inorganic). Repose is also quiet. And the sense of completion also arrives at a still point: "Nature would show you that all arrangement is organic and therefore complete in itself, and your work would have the repose which only a sense of completion can give... organic unity alone is noble and truly simple."[177] This is a very strange way to think of nature; a harmonious conclusion, not a process or even random change. But it can be related to the way architecture is founded on the spirit of elemental law and order presented in the 1908 essay. That historical goal is noble and truly simple. Simplicity is evident only after the "inessential" has been pared away. Changefulness, the trembling energy of nature, is to be seen past to a world of abstract perfection found in geometry.

Unity is a quality of nature only in the most abstracted view. Emerson's metaphor of the "angle of vision" illustrates this concept. At eye level there is only movement and variation. Only when you are way up, taking in a plan view of the world (where Wright finds the foundation of an architectural design), can you see the pattern that organizes the disparate parts into repose. For Wright, the plan is based on geometric abstract nature; the elevation is based on appearance. When Wright considers "the [ground plan] as a solution and [the elevation] an expression of the conditions of a problem," he is summarizing the whole project.[178]

The desired completeness Wright appeals to can only be found if you stop nature in its tracks. The "absolute repose which is of destiny fulfilled" sounds an awful lot like a mummy. The inevitability of decay, let alone growth, does appear to be expected by Wright, judging by the way his buildings are constructed. They are notoriously subject to decay, if not outright failure, owing to the willingness not to construct for the stillness of endurance.

The examples of nature that Wright consistently cites are quite specific and restricted. They are botanical, particularly trees, and surprisingly, crystals. The visible geometry of the latter explains their attraction. But Wright immediately circumscribes crystals' appearance with a warning about what their fixed geometry signifies: "All things in Nature exhibit this tendency to crystalize—to form and then conform..."[179] (Here is the geological alternative to nature as biology. Organic has two distinct characters for Wright, not always in harmony. There is an organic of resolution, a crystal stability, and an organic of evolution, a plant unfolding in time.) "This skeleton (mechanical requirement) rudiment accepted, *understood* is the first condition of any fruit or flower."[180] Here again the diagram is proposed as the first step. The clearest examples of these two aspects of organic are Unity Temple (1905–1907), and Taliesin (1911–1959). Unity Temple is stable and resolved (at least on first inspection) and Taliesin is about changes over time, evolution. The fact that these two buildings were designed six years apart testifies to Wright's understanding of organic's different aspects.

Even "crystallize" must be seen from more than one direction. When talking about "styles," Wright warns that it is dangerous when they crystallize. Culture changes. When it is stopped, crystallized, it loses all its creative potential. The attraction of the geometry of crystals is opposed by the fact that such patterns are the result of change, of time being stopped. If nature is anything, it is about change, evolution. He knows that the apparently contradictory forces of crystallization and growth have their respective point of contribution to human creative processes. "So this very useful tendency in the nature of the human mind, to standardize, is something to guard against as thought and feeling are about to take 'form'—something of which to beware—something to be watched."[181] A pattern then is transitory. The idea of pattern underlying appearance of nature can lead to a contradiction. Whatever stops growth opposes nature. The forces that stop the growth in the creation of architecture include the momentous repetition of the machine and the stability of the printed form of architecture.

ORGANIC

Organic is the other major slippery word in Wright's lexicon. For educational purposes, I have collected eleven pages of statements from Wright's writings that discuss the term organic. That goes to prove that it has as many aspects for Wright as the term nature, if not more. But all of them are intimately related. The boundary that distinguishes nature from organic is complex at an indeterminable level.

Here are a few quotations of Wright using the word organic:

1908 "To let individual elements arise and shine at the expense of final repose is, for the architect, a betrayal of trust....The work will become more plastic; more fluent, although more coherent; more organic."[182]

1914 "By organic architecture I mean an architecture that develops within outward in harmony with the condition of its being, as distinguished from one that is applied from without."[183]

1924 "The difference is all the difference between a thing

organic, complete in itself, and a patched composite, made and made regardless."[184]

1930 "The word 'organic' too, if taken too biologically, is a stumbling block."[185]

In the 1908 citation of *organic*, we have another example of Wright crossing over the meanings of categories in an effort to qualify what he is trying to say. "Final repose" is a resolution, a state arrived at after exerting the effort of design. "Fluent," flowing, is a way to describe change. (It is not possible to step into the same river twice.) But "coherent" is about things sticking together. The clue may lie in the subordinate conjunctive "although." In this proposition, *fluent* is the leader, *coherent* follows after. There is every reason to imagine that in another context the terms would be reversed. This sets up the possibility that change can be coherent. A second order of analysis would bypass the state of flowing to establish the pattern of flowing. That pattern could certainly be coherent. The state is looked past to see the process.

The various aspects of organic do share a crucial condition of harmony, of parts being generated from a given pattern. The alternative to organic growth in an ecological context is assemblage of parts imported from remote or alien contexts. Growing from within is one way Wright characterizes it, but that "within" includes, as he has asserted repeatedly, the mind that is cultivating the "within." The context includes the observer, a little like, if you will forgive me, the effect of observations in quantum mechanics.

Later Wright uses *organic* to refer to a variety of concepts, such as capitalism, a *thing of the heart*, and Gothic.[186] After characterizing a particular way to create architecture, it becomes a generic term of approbation and therefore less specific. That extension could account for the confusion over the term we see today. Is it still a useful term? I have my doubts.

The major internal boundary within Wright's organic is whether it is repose, a resolved arrangement of parts in a harmonious whole, like an observed natural artifact, or is it a process in time that engages change? These two characteristics of organic are not resolvable if considered concurrently. In the crossover pattern being presented here, we are asked to see botany as seen from crystals and from crystals looking at plants, each being the context for the other. It is possible to find the geometric patterns in diagrammatic abstractions of plants. And the temporal life of plants can be found in the process that results in molecules aligning in a crystal.

Wright finds a way to find both of these aspects when he is considering Louis Sullivan's ornament. "Terra cotta was this master's natural medium because his sense of beautiful form was the subtle fluctuation of flowering surface, song-like, as found in organic plant-life— the music of the crystal is seen as a minor accompaniment."[187] The crystal component may be minor when observing the finished ornament, but it is primary in setting out the armature on which the flowering expression can grow. When Sullivan composes his ornament in a sequence that begins with geometric diagram and concludes with the botanical imagery, both "organics" are in play. Looking at natural phenomena, seeing the organic of growth, is a process that "uncovers" the abstract pattern of the organic of crystals. Organic takes on the two characteristics at different times in the design and even in the use of an organic artifact. When resolution is important, the design of the organic artifact is like a crystal. When he needs to promote change, a plant, particularly a tree, is cited. The concurrence or sequence of resolved diagram and evolution of design makes Wright's "organic" difficult to bring into focus. Wright sees the geometric diagrams shown by a master Japanese print artist as a process employed to arrive at an image of the natural world that is resolved into a pattern of form and color that can be diagrammed. There is a process, a sequence in time that structures the appearances to embody the abstraction. "Hokusai textbooks wherein the structural diagrams are clearly given and transformation to material objects show progressively step by step."[188] Do the diagrams lead to the image, or does the image lead to the diagrams? It is likely, this being Frank Lloyd Wright, that it works coming and going.

Organic is flowering as structured by geometry. "There is a life-principle expressed in geometry at the center of every Nature-form we see. This integral pattern is abstract, lying within the object we see and that we recognize as concrete form....This hidden form-world is inherent in all forms. This form world is the architect's world. His thought must penetrate that world....The mind of the artist was touched by that form whatever it might be....Realism, now is as dead as realistic."[189] "The 'pictorial' still lives, for what it is...but as 'consequence' not as 'cause.'"[190]

Light has a different role in the two organics. When organic refers to nature as growth and change, light is valuable because it indicates depth and shadow. This shadowed light directed in a specific circumstance is the opposite of diffuse, indirect light that directs attention to the diagram underlying the appearances. "Organic architecture brings man once more face to face with nature's play of shade and depth of shadow seeing fresh vistas of native, creative human thought and native feeling presented to this imagination for consideration. That is modern."[191]

As Wright himself admitted, "The word 'organic' too, if taken too biologically, is a stumbling block. The word applies to 'living' structure—a structure or concept wherein features or parts are so organized in form and substance as to be, applied to purpose, 'integral.'"[192] The artifact that is structured by applying geometric abstraction is clearly not ultimately a fixed thing. Wright immediately puts the artifact to work. Time may seem to have been suspended in order to complete the commission, but it reenters the world of time when it is put to use. This alternation between resolution and evolution demonstrates how the complex boundary works but, more importantly, it emphatically establishes how and why Wright makes architecture.

HISTORY

For Wright, history shares with nature the characteristic that appearance can distract from "elemental law and order." If architectural examples from the past are taken literally as exemplars of form, as often they are in the academy, one never gets to that underlying order. Wright rejected the history that simply compiled form to be revered, copied, and rearranged. Architectural education in the academy was all about history. Recognition, connoisseurship, reproduction of historical monuments with ink washes constituted mastering the discipline that he saw representing the primary record of civilization. "American architects take their pick from the world's stock of 'ready-made' architecture and are most successful when transplanting form for form, line for line, enlarging details by means of lantern slides from photographs of the originals."[193] For Wright one side of history was "the constantly accumulating residue of formulas."[194] For Wright history was nutrient, not credential. He approached "nature" similarly. Both nature and history were important, not because citing them gave you authority but because their forms provided access to abstract order that produced form. Nature and history are lessons on how to make the connection between underlying principles and visible form, lessons an architect who aspires to something more than manipulation of form can benefit from.

Both history and convention have an internal boundary that separates the positive from the pejorative. When convention is applied to history, we know that it clarifies as well as constrains. In the opening paragraph of the 1908 "In the Cause of Architecture" essay, Wright clearly describes how after passing by the detritus of past architectural forms he looks back through their surfaces to the principles they embody. The historical architectural artifacts can be appreciated for their appealing compositions, but more importantly, they give access to and receive the love of the law and order that supports great architecture of their time. The temptation to take delight in the forms of historical buildings is dangerously parallel to the delight taken in the appearance of nature. That pleasure distracts from the more useful lessons that guide further actions. Resisting their siren calls is necessary to look beyond their delightful appearance to the laws that produced them. "Nothing is more difficult to achieve than the integral simplicity of organic nature amid the tangled confusions of the innumerable relics of form that encumber life for us."[195] Wright explicitly draws nature and history together. "The noble present," the site for action, eclipses the satisfaction of reposing in form.

After learning the conventions of architecture as he understood them in the early decades of the 20th century, the Oak Park Studio years, Wright began to characterize organic not as "complete in itself," but incorporating the effect of time. By the time his career entered a new phase in the 1930s, he threw over the poise of the classical in favor of an organic that was more identifiable with natural processes, particularly the passage of time. Symmetry and axes were attenuated or only hinted at. In a stunning qualification of that evolution, he writes in 1940 how he began his understanding of the discipline of architecture: "The 'academic' is the major and minor axis of classical architecture in human dress, or in human terms, which makes all symmetry a fixation." This is from an architect who clearly drew such axes in his plans in the Oak Park Studio years! "No chrysalis, this. At best we can see it as a crystal, and any crystal is a finality—fixation at the end of growth." But wait, there is a turn coming just when we think we understand the evolution of design goals to have become accepting, promoting(?) change: "[I]n Broadacres all is symmetrical, but it is seldom obviously and never academically so." This is newfound mastery, not repudiation. Symmetry, as in nature, or organic, or machine, have an internal boundary that is crossed over and seen from a direction conditioned by changes in his own mastery and the world which prompted the new viewpoint. Symmetry is now seen as a category that is useful only if it is a tool, not a goal. "I chose to break with traditions in order to be more true to Tradition than current conventions and ideals in architecture would permit."[196] He learned that from Sullivan: "What does it matter if Tradition's followers fail to see the Louis Sullivan's loyalty to traditions wholly complete and utterly profound? His loyalty was greater than theirs; as the Spirit transcends the Letter."[197]

He responded that the architecture he saw being constructed in the latter decades of the 19th century needed discipline. What needed discipline were the picturesque touches of C.F.A. Voysey, Edwin Lutyens, and C.R. Ashbee, among others. Although discipline for Wright did not mean Lutyens' capitulation to classicism, it stimulated Wright's powerful interpretive powers. The classical revival of the 1890s in American architecture provided a system to organize the delights of formal invention. As Henry Russell Hitchcock observed in his 1944 essay, "Frank Lloyd Wright and the 'Academic Tradition' of the Early Eighteen-nineties," Wright had digested that discipline more subtly than most.[198] "The academic ideal, accepted by Wright in its fashionable surface forms for only a year or two, creatively modified…" by him subsequently, became the basis of his own architecture.[199] Of all the up-and-coming young architects in Chicago, why did Daniel Burnham offer to send Wright to the École des Beaux-Arts in Paris? Wright used classical "syntax" without classical vocabulary, although he did demonstrate his understanding of classical syntax in his entry for the Milwaukee Library competition. In his search for armatures to stabilize the changes in nature and in culture, Wright found geometry and how it was used in selected examples from history. The conventional armature of classical architecture, the order of the past, when seen beyond the specific forms accumulated in history, provided orderliness that helped structure architecture, particularly when he was acquiring the skills to become an architect.

For an aspiring American architect to go to Japan before Europe is an unmistakable assertion of an unconventional response to history. Tokyo before Paris is a bold stand for a thirty-something architect from the Midwest. "Owing to its marked eccentricity this art [of Japan] is a particularly safe means of cultivating for us because the individual initiative of the artist is not paralyzed by forms which he can use as he finds them readymade."[200] Historical forms ready-made in the Western canon were expected to underlie the practice of architecture. Wright's appreciation of Japan may have resulted in some more literal responses, but its unfamiliarity for most in the West meant he could refer to it with some impunity. Of course, his claim that Japan confirmed his goals would mean that he was prepared to "see" Japan, not just discover it.

Wright reacted to the contemporary architecture coming out of Europe in much the same way he reacted to historical architecture. Wright responds to the contemporary characterizations of his work as "neither 'New' nor 'Old' just pioneering, that's all, groundbreaking and sound."[201] After castigating the influence of French architectural fashion of "surface and mass," he finds in its origins a "[l]ean, hard plainness, mistaken for simplicity, [that] has the quality of simplicity to a refreshing extent, where all is fat or false. It is aristocratic, by contrast."[202] That sentence doubles back on itself more than once. Simplicity is generally good, but can be mistaken, presumably, as empty. But it can serve as a refreshing antidote to the squishiness of falsity. And then the American democrat casts a brief approving glance at the "aristocratic." It is all in how you look at it and Wright looks right and left, back and forth seeing differences and similarities evident from different perspectives.

DEMOCRACY

Probably the most notorious category where Wright seems to be talking out of both sides of his mouth is democracy. As an American architect, Wright stands for democracy, the practice that separated the United States from the Old World. In *When Democracy Builds* (the 1945 rewrite of the 1932 *The Disappearing City*), the title of his proposition for inhabiting the land, Wright makes repeated citations of the need for Americans to chart a new course for culture and architecture that rejected the aristocratic old world in order to embrace the new democratic world. "The Machine [i]s the forerunner of Democracy" is another surprising crossover of values.[203] These propositions celebrated what Wright dedicated his architecture to. Wright also saw the negative aspect of the democracy he came to call "mobocracy." Which side of the line is Wright's true position? Of course, by now, we know the answer isn't found in either location but in the journey crossing over the boundary to see both sides.

Like so many things Wright took positions on, democracy was internally partitioned by conflicting forces. It was not a condition but an ideal that had the potential to foster excellence that could come from anywhere. The challenge, of course, was not to have those who achieved excellence claim permanent privilege for having done so. For Wright, excellence was the goal; what suppressed it in favor of some form of equality or frustrated it by lack of recognition were roundly rejected. "When it is understood that a great Democracy is the highest form of Aristocracy conceivable, not of birth or place or wealth, but of those qualities that give distinction to the man as a man, and that as a social state it must be characterized by the honesty and responsibility of the absolute individualist as the unit of its structure, then only can we have an art worthy of name."[204]

This statement, found in the second paper "In the Cause of Architecture" of 1914, is part of the commentary by Wright that is less about architecture and more about the social/professional context he was contending with at the end of the halcyon days of the Oak Park Studio. It is so representative of how he addresses a category with internal contradictions. Actually, that is not the right assessment. It is not so much about contradictions in a category or between categories but how they embody the indisputable fact that they are not unitary. They are not contradictory; their conflicts are not struggles seeking dominance but the effort seeking to qualify each other. Just like *radical* and *conservative* in the 1908 "In the Cause of Architecture," *democracy* and *aristocracy* are not opposites but qualifying forces whose interaction over the complex boundary where they meet creates a greater level of understanding. There is no question, however, that Wright falls into the perennial trap that one's own excellence apparently entitles permanent status as he looked down from the hilltop architect's retreat above his imagined Broadacre City.

The "responsibility of the absolute individualist" sums up how complex this interaction really is. "This dream of freedom, as voiced by the Declaration of Independence, is dear to the heart of everyman who has caught the spirit of American institutions; therefore the ideal of every man American in feeling and spirit. Individuality is a national ideal. Where this degenerates into petty individualism, it is but a manifestation of weakness in the human nature, and not a fatal flaw in the ideal."[205]

As an American democrat, Wright leads with the individual's freedom to develop his own potential. Forces that frustrate or fail to cultivate that potential are precisely what America sought to flee from the overdeveloped structures of European culture. But no sooner is the primacy of the individual posited than Wright crosses over to the side of democracy that requires responsibility to contribute to the whole. The individual, like the raw expression of nature, can only acquire the power to build in the world by going through the process of conventionalization, the patterns that provide the context for the striking vitality of the individual. "[T]he true Democrat takes the human flower as it grows, and in the spirit of using the means at hand, he puts Life into his conventionalization— preserves the individuality of the flower which is his life—getting from it a living expression of its essential character, fitted perfectly to its place, without loss of vital significance."[206] Wright brings the two aspects of the category *democracy* together by identifying individuality, not as a sui generis condition, but the individual response to the context in which it finds itself. Individuality is the result of universal principles expressed in a specific context. "Time and place are conditions, are the limitations within which—yes, by means of which—individuality is born."[207] This is a profound reflection on the shortcomings of absolute categories or thinking. The challenge is always to work the connection, the complex boundaries where different aspects meet. That is where architecture takes place for Wright. It is neither either/or nor both/and. Each apparent relation between differences does not express how a static condition or a permissive truce actually engenders the continuous interaction of differences that fuel any creative activity, particularly of architecture.

The individual seen from the perspective of the larger, underlying pattern is different from the individual's perspective looking over to conventionalization. From that side, conventionalization is constraining and a source of frustration. The individual taking their place in a "harmonious whole" sums up the continuous reflection that is the practice of democracy. "[O]ur ideal is Democracy, the highest possible expression of the individual as a unit not inconsistent with a harmonious whole."[208] That consistency is not a static state but a workshop for creation.

Bringing "architecture" to people beyond princes and bishops is what an American architecture would be for Wright. The means that the history of architecture used, no, the principles that underlay the specific manifestations, are still to be respected, not erased. American architecture would be a principled continuity with the spirit of architecture, but its manifestations would be our own. Wright was not proposing to plant his architecture in barren land cleared by cultural weedkiller of all precedents. History is another source if one knows how to use it.

This brief review of how Wright discussed topics related to his thinking about architecture displays the pattern of crossing complex boundaries. Whenever he cites a category, he almost immediately qualifies the initial statement, seeing it from an alternative, often opposing estimation. He seems particularly wary of taking a singular stand, and when it seems he is doing so, it draws attention not to a singular understanding but to a complex one. As I mentioned above, he is not an effective partisan except for a habit of thought and design that embraces boundaries to be crossed. Is this posture just caution, a slippery avoidance of commitment? I would suggest not. The goal is abundance—

he cites the English mystic artist/poet William Blake for this, writing, "Good William Blake says exuberance is beauty"—not reductive clarity.[209] When he recommends looking for the underlying abstraction of nature, it is not to overcome or set aside the richness of visible nature, only to interpret that abundance in favor of further, creative production. More work! Reducing sources, whether visual, conceptual, or historical, simply constricts possibilities. Wright's reticence to trace in words his design process simply indicates that he wants to get on with designing, not explaining. His writings rarely tell how he came up with his designs. They are loftier commentaries on general principles. That is why he says he is not a teacher; he is an architect busy with designing. If you want to learn, watch.

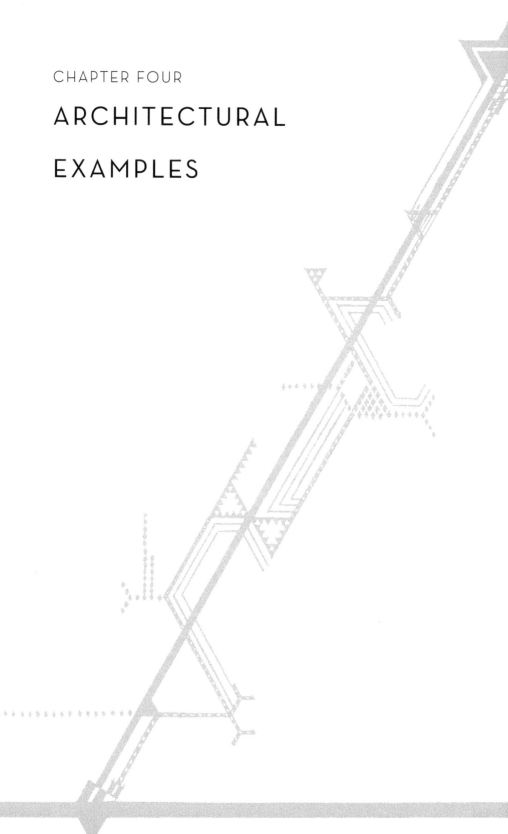

CHAPTER FOUR

ARCHITECTURAL
EXAMPLES

This narrative followed a pattern of boundaries in Frank Lloyd Wright's buildings and writings characterized as complex. The consequence for architecture poses a question: what is the point of making complex boundaries in a building? Drawing clear, absolute distinctions, separating one place or condition with a knife-edge difference from another has its appeal, to be sure. You always know where you are and where you are not. That clarity frees up energy and attention that would otherwise be required to decide your location. If the circumstances where the distinction between being inside or out require decisive action, there is no time for mulling and wondering. In any circumstance that threatens basic survival, decisiveness is appropriate. An architecture of peace and plenty can step away from threats to survival that rely on absolute distinctions to make complex boundaries that incorporate more functions and formal potentials. This discussion of Frank Lloyd Wright's architecture proposes that something is gained by boundaries that are not absolute, that are not constructed as single planes of separation. Such boundaries can extend human experience and use.

In a lecture at Columbia University in 1966, Peter Pragnell, a British member of Team Ten, a successor to CIAM (Congres Internationaux d'Architecture Moderne), presented an image of Wright's Taliesin West that showed walls and terraces reaching out into the desert surroundings. He characterized this as "architecture with diarrhea." As a brash undergraduate, I seethed with resentment, waiting for the riposte that would defeat his attack. He handed it to me on a silver platter by showing a Unite d'Habitation by Le Corbusier, saying it did not have diarrhea; "No," I replied, "it has constipation!" The Unites are tightly contained rectangular blocks elevated from the ground, standing free of their context. Pragnell's point was that clear separations were something architecture was supposed to establish. Le Corbusier's high school art teacher, Charles L'Eplattenier, presented a pedagogy from an Arts and Crafts perspective. In fact, early drawings of ornament by Le Corbusier have a lot in common with Wright's ornamental studies. Charles-Edouard

Jeanneret-Gris, before he restyled himself with a definite article when he was thirty, had to make a choice as he set off from the confines of Switzerland to embrace a larger world. To claim his place in the privileged classical culture of France, the only country in Europe spanning from the northern world of Arts and Crafts to the classical Mediterranean, he headed south. His definition of architecture—"*L'architecture est le jeu savant, correct et magnifique des volumes assembles sous la lumiere*" ("Architecture is the masterful, correct, and wonderful play of volumes assembled under the light")—is worlds away from misty, northern forests.[210]

The singular volume, in shadowless distinction, clearly bounded from context, depicted in Le Corbusier's Purisme still-lifes, were Greek temples sitting proudly on a geological prominence. We remember Corbusier's straight path up the hill in contrast to Wright's crisscrossing path in the snow in order to gather weeds! Singular, distinctive clarity compared to complex engagement with possibilities.

The posture taken by human beings in opposition to the world they find themselves in is a heroic gesture of defiance and self-definition embracing a tragic worldview. To cite Vincent Scully, Yale architectural historian: "Taliesin West is therefore not a Hellenic exploration of the tragic balance between man and nature but a simple recognition by man of nature's engrossing power and a ceremonial submission of himself to it." Wright's architecture "avoid[s] reference to the human body… [it] abstract[s] the natural environment…"[211] Classical sculpture of the human body parallels the Greek temple as described by Scully's poetic evocation of its singular gesture in the landscape and is substantially at odds with Wright's alternative view of human life. His view builds on an acknowledgment, even an embrace, of interdependence. Whatever tragedy there is for Wright's position in the world, it is not the classical retribution visited on humans by the world they did not make. It is a more poignant recognition that every human act, regardless of its position in the world, will always generate opposition or conflict. Singing about this difference, the lyrical alternative to the tragic, celebrates art instead of hubris. Wright's constructional methods challenge best practices that are directed to build a more enduring boundary with the environment—think roof leaks. Such constructional laxity may seem an arrogant, contrary posture, but because any construction is susceptible to change, although inconvenient at times, Wright's buildings almost always call out for continuous, even initial, maintenance. Carefree construction was never the goal. Living with a building that requires attention, sometimes constant, engages the inhabitant with architecture whether they signed on to do that or not. The classical arrogance of the isolated figure is more a symbol than a way to build, as it attempts to challenge its earthbound condition and inevitably fails.

The complex boundaries of Frank Lloyd Wright do not engage human life and experience by means of clear and absolute distinctions. Nor do they embrace ambiguity for its own sake, just to be perverse in an avant garde, *épater la bourgeoisie* (befuddle the shopkeepers) gesture. Complex architectural perimeters simulate the reality of not only the vagaries of daily life but embrace change and evolution rather than assert immutability.

The buildings Frank Lloyd Wright designed and built have a distinctive complexity in the boundaries with their context. The complexity of those boundaries can be described using the words Wright appropriated from Louis Sullivan's characterization of his ornament: continuity and plasticity. Wright's repeated citation of these descriptions of his architecture's formal aspect reinforces the connection between architecture and ornament. When considering the perimeter boundary of a building, recognizing that the separation between inside and out is the point of the construction, that relation takes on a wide range of constructional patterns. If the context is or can be modulated to be less threatening, the separation can be minimal; if it is hostile, many materials may be combined to make the inside habitable. Wright's two Taliesins demonstrate this difference quite clearly. A house of the north as Wright described his home/studio in Wisconsin has walls of stone, wood, plaster, roofs of shingles, and openings filled with glass both openable and fixed. Taliesin West, a winter campsite in the Sonoran Desert of Arizona, is constructed of boundaries that are quite permeable. Wooden screens and movable flaps, roofs of canvas imply boundaries that minimally separate inside from out, especially between the buildings. The spaces between the pavilions of Taliesin West are another boundary where the outside is not quite outside but modified places not wholly architecture and not wholly nature. By these means the requirements of human habitation are served quite differently by boundaries that are not defensive. After all, Taliesin West was established as a camp for 70-year-old Wright to escape the winter weather in Wisconsin. Wright saw a camp and picnics as necessary reminders of architecture's place in the natural world.

Following an ancient tradition, Wright's desert and California buildings are predominantly wall architecture, while his northern buildings are roof constructions. These categories describe the distinction between Mediterranean and northern forest architecture from time immemorial. Climate and building materials are interrelated; masonry of mud or stone contrasted to roofs of wood. Therein lie two significant determinants for buildings: bearing walls and cantilevers. Each method produces different ways of displaying continuity and plasticity. In wall architectures, the complex boundary is developed in plan, since the roof is drawn into the perimeter rather than projecting out, owing to the structural spans between bearing walls. While in roof architecture, the distinctive boundary manipulation occurs in section as well, which adds roof projections to the variation in wall configuration of projection and recess.

The crossover form produces projections and recesses along the perimeter of a building. Walls are not simple, straight lines, but turn and return to create the plasticity of Sullivan's ornament. When the wall was to open from inside to out, Wright asserted that "there were to be no holes cut in wall as holes are cut in a box, because this was not in keeping with the ideal of 'plastic.'"[212] An opening called for a modulation in depth of the perimeter. In section the projection/recess is also carried out by horizontal planes overhead and underfoot. The cantilever, usually accomplished with linear structural members of wood (or later steel) is the primary means to create the plasticity of perimeter in the vertical dimension. When the horizontal roofs and vertical projections of walls and pavements are not aligned, when their respective perimeters project and recess independently, further boundary complexity results.

Plasticity is evident in the projections/recesses outlined above. Continuity describes how the distinctions between inside and out are expanded and made ambiguous. Ambiguity may be a critical way to describe this formal condition. The plasticity is actually in service to continuity as the boundary condition is made "thick." The projections and recesses modify the transition so continuity between inside and out is incremental, not abrupt. Expanding the abstract plane of a boundary condition adds Wright's highly valued "third dimension" as the forms and surfaces perpendicular to the plane of separation link the inside and outside visually and through human passage. The third dimension has a formal function, but it also constructs the human movement across the boundary as more than a single step.

Frank Lloyd Wright's buildings are not just artifacts in an exterior context. The same qualities of complex boundaries appear on the interiors. The concept of "space" used by Wright and others to describe what his architecture has that other architecture lacks is fundamentally a quality defined by the continuity and plasticity of the boundaries of the interior. Space is only perceived because of its limits. Wright's interior enclosures combine continuity from room to room, if that common term is even applicable, and plasticity as ceilings and balconies cantilever, as floor levels rise and fall. The emphasis in this review focuses on the boundaries between the building and its context, but the same exploration applies to the interiors as some are examined in the following examples.

The image of crossing over boundaries was proposed to a few architecture undergraduates in the drafting room of the Columbia University School of Architecture in 1966. The esteemed and elegant Serge Chermayeff (1900–1996), a leader in British modern architecture, was hanging out with us on his trip to New York from his visiting professorship at Yale. He shared with us how he had come to think of architecture like an iceberg: 10 percent visible above the water and 90 percent invisible below the water. He now thought the parts of architecture like economy, sociology, philosophy, etc., the non-visible context that supports architecture, were the most important. As a cheeky youth who thought architecture's unique role was choosing form, I begged to differ with his eminence. I replied that the important part of architecture was the waterline, the point where the invisible became visible; that was where the real work was done. He gave me a look, but not a word, that recognized (I decided to think!) I had a point. A metaphor I used later was how like the newt an architect had to be; an amphibian who continually crossed over that waterline breathing in the watery darkness only to cross over to breathe in the light and air.

The waterline image concentrates the question posed by this narrative: what are the bases for decisions about form? What content is brought over from the invisible to the visible that contributes to making choices about the form of a building? There is an unsolvable mystery here, of course. The way form is chosen remains locked up in the mind of the artist or architect. There are ways to approach this question, some more grounded in example, some simply stories created by historians or critics purporting to think like the architect. The present narrative proposes that when Wright's writings are set beside his buildings, we may discern how the non-visible patterns of thought and words below the waterline lead to architectural patterns visible above the waterline. Stepping beyond the context of Wright's mind as reported in his writings, there is the larger context of history, precedents, cultural conditions, all the forces and circumstances that condition the choice of form. This context is describable in some detail, texts and images surround an architect's designing. Proposing how they are carried across the boundary to guide the choice of form is a challenging task often reduced to seeing things from the context that look like the artifact under examination. Cause and effect are ultimately elusive. The possibility of finding hints does exist, however. That is why I began with the graphic of Wright walking up the hill in the snow with Uncle John. Here is a visible pattern that seems to be aligned with a way of thinking that results in a way of forming. By creating and featuring this form, Wright may be indicating how he crossed and recrossed the waterline as he made choices of form.

These crossover points might be seen as the crux of architectural design. The plan of a building lays out continuity as one moves past parts of the perimeter before actually crossing the boundary to the inside. Piers, porches, knee-walls, planters, paving all expand the boundary condition experientially as well as functionally. The way people congregate at doorways is an indication of how compelling the intermediate location is. Crossing over in section is the primary function of Wright's beloved cantilever. The space under the cantilever is not wholly outside nor inside. It is the perfect structural means to expand the boundary between inside and out.

Ceilings and roofs are also architectural elements where boundaries can be made complex. Producing vertical projections and recesses in the water-shedding element of a roof is probably the origin of the leaky roof phenomenon in Wright lore. As Wright established himself in his early career, the familiar hipped roof of the Prairie period is part of the tradition of constructional stability. However, their minimal slope may be seen as a concession to water shedding in the effort to achieve the desired formal horizontality. The ceilings of the Oak Park Studio houses achieve complex boundaries between vertical and horizontal planes by means of wood stripping and continuous color of ceiling and wall. Wright stretched conventional construction at the intersections of roofs with masonry masses when he left out flashing because it interrupted the formal composition of masses and planes. The various levels of flat roofs and clerestories of the Usonian houses create complex spatial boundaries by introducing light from above. When ceilings move up and down in these Usonian dwellings, the joints in the water-shedding surfaces set up the admission of not only light but water.

After looking for crossover patterns that create complex boundaries in prose, in categories of thought, between ornament and structure, now for an examination of Frank Lloyd Wright's buildings seen as boundaries being crossed. This is, of course, the whole point in considering the work of an architect. This way of looking at Wright's architecture parallels previous observations made by many others of his buildings: bringing the outside in, flowing interior spaces, compression-release, architecture continuous with nature. The boundary-crossing pattern proposed here seeks to be somewhat more general and explanatory. Those more familiar descriptions of what is characteristic of Wright's architecture recognize how building and site, room and room are separated and linked by architectural features that create complexity by projections and recesses. The present expansion of these descriptions focuses on the composition of the material boundaries that link and separate, that cross over and back. Human use, function, direct this pattern, but perception and formal composition contribute as well. We move and we look and listen and respond haptically.

To return to the key terms, continuity and plasticity, from the discussion of ornament and Louis Sullivan, we found their initial material realization in ornament. Continuity described how the ornament was not separate from its base or its setting. It was not "on" something but "of" it. The continuity was constructed by the ordering pattern that connected the distinct parts. Plasticity described the projection/recession of the elements that constituted the ornament. The ornament projects and recedes to create depth in three dimensions.

A recurring image Wright uses to describe his architecture is weaving. "All the buildings I have built—large and small—are fabricated upon a unit system—as the pile of a rug is stitched into the warp."[213] The long fibers of the warp run through the loom and are crossed by the weft going back and forth through the warp threads. The warp and the weft are at right angles to each other creating an orthogonal structure. The warp is continuous, rolled up at both ends and pulled along as the weft alternates up and down through the warp. The weft is usually the means to create pattern. (Some Chinese silk weaves use the weft to bring out the pattern in the warp, however, and recent experiments in three-dimensional fabrics have expanded this traditional image of weaving.) The horizontal plane of the warp is raised into a shallow third dimension by the weft. Continuity and a crossing pattern create an enmeshing geometry within which one can imagine a building being designed and constructed. Wright's geometry—whether orthogonal, "reflex" (30/60 angles), or circular/radial—weaves his architecture together. Its unmistakably "woven" quality established continuities within the artifact and the context without. It is distinctly different from architecture taking its origin in bodies, especially the human figure. Wright's geometrization of nature is not applied to donkeys or man, for that matter; it is plants or crystals.

Weaving can be correlated with architecture on several points. The freedom of design residing in the weft depends on the continuity of the warp to hold it together. The continuous regularity of the warp is the discipline making that freedom possible. The geometric field the warp sets up also has a repetitive module that connects with a unit system. The weft moves perpendicular to the warp and thereby traces a plane that intersects it. In a metaphorical leap I hope you can survive, it may be possible to associate the warp with hypotaxis, the perspectival continuity that recedes from the perceptual present of the parataxis of the weft.

Wright's appreciation of the Gothic as opposed to the Renaissance may have its basis in the linear patterns of colonnettes, and moldings. The Gothic creates structures whose outlines, whose perimeters are not clearly bound; they project with crockets, buttresses, and sculpture all linearly connected.

The two structural systems that Frank Lloyd Wright employs to separate his vision of architecture from the "solid cube carved" by Western architectural tradition are the cantilever and the structural plane. The cantilever is a horizontal form while the structural plane is primarily a vertical form. Together they create an architecture that departs significantly from historical precedents because they enable crossing boundaries in ways that carving does not. A roof cantilever covers an area that is not clearly inside the perimeter wall and is not clearly outside either. The same goes for interior cantilevers that create a space that is shared by two adjacent spaces. Wright's various citations of the cantilever's structural function or efficiency minimizes its central role in crossing boundaries. A striking difference between Sullivan and Wright beyond their respective interpretations of ornament's function and potential is how Sullivan dismisses the cantilever and Wright embraces it for the very same reasons. Sullivan identifies "three elementary forms, the pier, the lintel and the arch."[214] In *Kindergarten Chats* he puts the cantilever in its place, the very place that Wright's architecture exploits. For Sullivan the cantilever "is not primary. It belongs among those secondary structural forms which may be classed as expedients. It is neither one thing nor the other; neither pier, lintel nor arch though it seems curiously to partake of their functions in a reverse or imitative way. It may assist pier, lintel and arch. Its essence is overhang. The pier, lintel and arch are in their simplest forms primary propositions. The cantilever belongs in the province of morphology."[215] Wright's study of forms took him way beyond Sullivan's elementary forms to an architecture that reveled in being "neither one thing nor the other." For him, "the cantilever became a new feature in architecture....Slabs stiffened and used over supports as cantilevers to get planes parallel to the earth, such as were now necessary to develop emphasis of the third dimension."[216]

The structural plane's contribution to this architectural goal is more complicated. Its flexibility as supporting structure frees up the relation of inside and out from the cage-like regularity of the post-and-beam system and supports interior spaces that "flow." With the use of reinforced concrete, Wright is able to fold structural planes in both horizontal and vertical dimensions.

Boundary crossing occurs at small and large scales in Wright's work: buildings and site, interior/exterior, room to room. Openings of doors and windows are the first place to look. Section drawings of the walls of any building show how the construction of openings requires detailed attention. Moldings have always been developed at these locations whether classical, medieval, Renaissance, or modern (which reveled in minimizing the detailing at those points potentially to assert that separations can be abstractly suppressed.)

The selection of Wright's buildings presented here is intentionally only suggestive. The goal is not a comprehensive review, but it is hoped others can use them to initiate exploration of other examples with this proposition in mind. Of course, the buildings are chosen to advance the proposition that complex boundaries are part of Wright's unique contribution to architecture.

The first buildings used here to demonstrate architectural boundary crossing are the Stockman House (1908) in Iowa and the Evans House (1908) in Illinois. The main elevation of the living rooms shows the complexity of wall and windows as various architectural elements cross over a simple, implied boundary projecting inside and out. Projections from the plane of the enclosing wall accommodate windows but also indicate how the boundary is expanded for functional and perceptual reasons. The contrast between the uninterrupted walls next to the windows and the profile of the windows exemplifies the effort Wright exercises to construct and signify

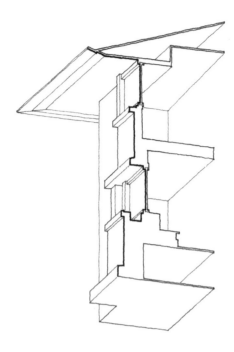

Figure 4.1. G. C. Stockman House, Mason City, Iowa. Wall section.
(Drawing by Patrick Kinsfather)

the openings (figs. 4.1, 4.2). From the exterior, the frames and cantilevering
"shelves" echo the deep roof cantilever at the top of the wall. This extended
plane overhead protects the material of the wall, but it emphatically sets up
the shelter of human activity underneath. If one posits a sequence of vertical
planes moving toward the house the first element encountered is the edge
of the roof. Step by step the next element encountered is the planter box at
the base of the wall. And then the edges of the frames and shelves around
the windows are touched and at last we are through the enclosing plane
and have arrived inside. Working the other way from the inside, the density
of these horizontal projections finally gives way to the last element, the
roof edge. These projections create planes at right angles to the wall plane.
They protect the opening and reconfigure the wall material that has been

CROSSING BOUNDARIES WITH FRANK LLOYD WRIGHT

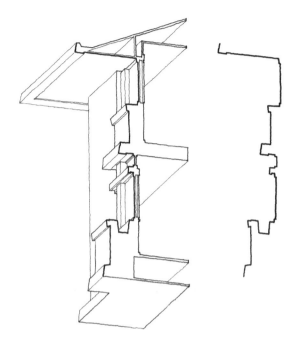

Figure 4.2. Raymond W. Evans House, Chicago. Wall section.
(Drawing by Patrick Kinsfather)

peeled back to make the opening. They are the weft, the three-dimensional depth that reaches out from the inside to the outside. The planting boxes concentrate the botanical nature up close. From the inside these projections expand the horizontal planes of ceiling and floor, the surfaces sheltering the people inside. They expand the interior visually, so separation is not abrupt. They mitigate the boundary that is at once desired and modified. Looking from outside, then looking from inside, the complex boundary elements create a deep frame to connect to the exterior and an expansive reach from inside to out. It is clear now why Wright rejected double-hung, or guillotine windows as he castigated them, which open by sliding within the plane of the wall, in favor of casement windows, whose cantilever projections when opened create another boundary-crossing element.

Figure 4.3. Emil Bach House, Chicago.
(Photograph by Sidney K. Robinson)

CROSSING BOUNDARIES WITH FRANK LLOYD WRIGHT

The projections around the openings in these two houses can also be seen as formal play not unlike ornament. They rise from the larger context of volumes found at the perforations where people move in and out of the houses and reinforce the activity and the perception of crossing boundaries. The delight in formal patterns, particularly in the third dimension, as demonstration of plasticity, looked for ways to be activated. Finding connections between that formal activity and functional use and human perception is what makes Wright's architecture so engaging.

The Bach House (1915) in Chicago can almost be seen as habitable ornament; its perimeter boundary projects and recesses considerably more than its familiar "Fire Proof House for $5,000" plan would suggest (fig. 4.3). The approach to the house directs path and views in five changes of direction. The projections that surround the basic square plan create the complex boundary in the horizontal plane. The entrance projection is a self-contained, pavilion-like unit; the front projection of the house extends the central axis, which is unexpectedly at right angles to the fireplace, and the rear extensions are generated by the stair and the porch originally accessing views of Lake Michigan. The extensions in the horizontal plane appear as various levels of cantilevers emphasizing the cross-axial plan sitting on top of the square base. These upper-level cantilevers make the boundaries around the windows an ornamental pattern loosely related to window construction and maximally related to making the upper-floor boundary a significantly more complex opening to the exterior than the masonry walls of the first floor. There is not just one projection of the roof over the windows, the window bands have their own small eyebrows. These window "boxes" not only have their own cantilevers on top, they are visually supported at the bottom by planes that extend beyond their edges. The boundary of the top level of the Bach House is clearly complex for formal reasons. Closed versus open, solid versus penetrable, calm versus animated are all expressed in this house as ornament.

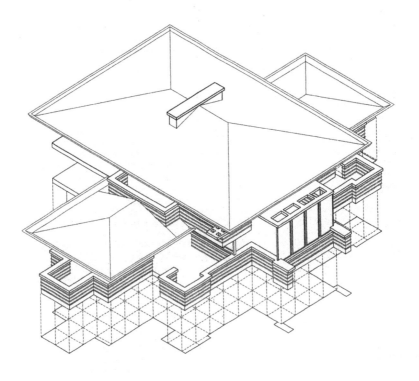

Figure 4.4. Emily and George C. Stewart House, Montecito, California.
(Drawing by Thad Trejo)

Considering larger, volumetric activity, the Stewart House (1909) in California is an amazing exercise of roofs, balconies, and windows crossing from inside to outside (figs. 4.4–4.7). If we start with the simple idea that a building is an envelope that intervenes between the world surrounding the place marked out for human habitation and the modified, conditioned world that is being requested to enable, encourage, and enhance human activities, the simplest boundary is a plane, vertical and horizontal. We find that Wright's architecture is not enclosed by simple planes, but by a series of projections inward and outward from the initial defining boundary. Whether we characterize that expansion as thick section or thick narrative as we construct the boundary for functional, perceptual, or aesthetic purposes, the result increases the

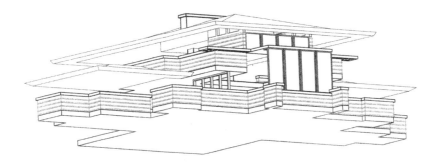

Figure 4.5. Emily and George C. Stewart House.
(Drawing by Thad Trejo)

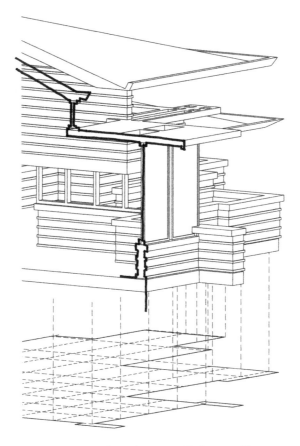

Figure 4.6. Emily and George C. Stewart House.
(Drawing by Thad Trejo)

Figure 4.7. Emily and George C. Stewart House. Perspective.
Plate XLIIIa, Stewart House (detail), *Ausgeführte Bauten und Entwürfe*,
Berlin: E. Wasmuth, 1910. Avery Classics, Avery Architectural and
Fine Arts Library, Columbia University.

dimension crossing that plane. This increased dimension usually takes some orthogonal pattern of projections from the vertical plane as we engage and reach out from the conditioned volume and as we bring in, through visibility and perforations, the surrounding context. Architecture can be seen as the story told about the boundaries we make around our lives and the world in which we live them. Not all architectures aspire to that complexity.

The part of the Stewart House to be examined is the living room and the second-floor bedroom balconies alongside it. The front of the living room is a wonderfully complex set of projections and recessions that make determining when you have crossed the boundary from inside to out, not aggravating, but an exciting exploration. Starting from the ground outside the tall windows we first encounter, in a series of sections working almost as a weft crossing back and forth over the warp of the building, a planter bounded by two short piers. This preparation for the building organizes the natural context through architectural geometry. These piers are not square or round, but rectangular, projecting out from the implied enclosing planes. This pier form, whose sides are perpendicular to the abstraction of the building's enclosing walls, set up the outreaching linkages of the complex boundary. I proposed in an earlier essay that the Prairie School can be characterized by a preference for "domino" shaped elements, especially piers whose minor faces to the outside and inside are connected by major surfaces perpendicular to the enclosing boundary plane.[217]

Once past the planter box we encounter the tall window wall capped by a flat roof which, in turn, supports a higher row of windows at its interior edge. These windows are not just in the front plane, at a lower level, they turn the corner to complete the volume set by the roof. Over the lower, flat roof we meet the cantilevered ledge of the main roof of the whole room. Now things get intensely "plastic." That means that there are several enclosure planes vertical (walls and windows), horizontal (ceilings and roofs), crossing inside and out. From the outside the complex enclosure makes the encounter with the building not abrupt and oppositional but the presentation of several points of "entry." As a rural retreat, these projections and recessions make the boundary between building and natural context a multidimensional connection of view, balcony, interior.

From the inside there are variations in how the enclosure is conditioned by multiple readings of how that separation is achieved. The goal is not to blur the boundary but to articulate it by plastic projections and recesses in the service of continuity between inside and out. That plasticity, that projection/recess directs interpretation of the relationships between the two because the difference is not singular but multiple. This description at the scale of a building directly parallels the description of ornament presented earlier. One of the most effective ways to achieve this entwining of continuity and plasticity is being able to see part of the extended building from wherever you are. Cantilevered roofs, projecting planters, frames bent around corners engage inhabitant and setting in multiple ways.

These extensions are made by having the planes made by walls and windows fold perpendicularly to themselves, thus prolonging the trip from inside to outside. This material continuity cutting across the enclosing boundary is found in the row of windows beginning to the side of the large window wall and turning along the length of the room. The ceiling over this lower band of windows extends outside to become the floor of the sleeping balcony for the second-floor bedrooms. To carry the tall wall over this band of windows, this high plane is supported from a wooden truss hidden in the roof of the whole room. This hidden structure holds up one edge of the balcony floor that is balanced on the wall of the lower band of windows. Not being able to easily read the means of support dramatizes how the structure crosses the boundaries of enclosure and of interior spaces. Uncertainty of support and boundaries of enclosure work together to achieve Wright's way of separating and linking categories. Further extensions occur from the balcony over the fireplace which gives access to the bedrooms. These bedrooms have floors that create the ceiling at the entry to the first level porch and dining room and, like the tall windows at the front of the living room, reach out to the edge of the main roof which cantilevers beyond the edges of the bedrooms' exterior balconies. Trying to determine where the ultimate enclosure for the house actually lies requires shifting perspectives and interpretations of just what enclosure means. This house is a dramatic demonstration of Wright crossing boundaries as continuity and plasticity animate and challenge perception from inside and out. At points, the view outside is capped by a cantilever, at other points the window's top frame is at the edge of the roof. And at still other locations the viewpoint outside floats between a cantilevering roof and cantilevering balcony floor.

Another example of such boundary complexity is found at the celebrated Boynton House (1908) dining room. Again, starting outside from the planting box, the next plane is the row of windows that constitute a kind of conservatory with a low flat roof that supports a band of windows for a higher-ceilinged dining room (fig. 4.8). What makes this band intriguing is that it lights a narrow slot backed by the lower wall of the second-floor bedrooms, whose windows create a third band set back again. From the exterior, trying to determine the enclosure of this "wall" of the house is a great puzzlement. The receding vertical planes and the connecting horizontal planes contribute to an ambiguity of what spaces are being contained. This ambiguity, delightful and curious, is immediately encountered upon entering the house (figs. 4.9, 4.10). Straight ahead from the front door one sees into the dining room, through a window, across an intervening exterior space to another window cantilevered from the lowest band of windows as a kind of glass box and out again to the exterior. It is extravagant, to be sure, but a more intense demonstration of boundary crossing is hard to imagine.

A far less playful, even earnest in its tight composition, example is the Robie House (1908-1910). The boundary crossing here is prominent in the extensive cantilever from the end of the living room over the raised terrace (fig. 4.11). This deep, "captured" space between the floor and the smooth plane of the soffit is dramatic, but its power comes from the ambiguity of enclosure. If one measures the distance from the edge of the terrace, then the marvelous knife-edge of the copper enclosed gutter above, then the point of the window that marks the final enclosure, you have traveled some 20 feet. This depth is made possible by an important structural model Wright used early and often. The extent of the cantilever when read from the edge of the roof back to the pier at the end of the row of French doors along the front of the house, is truly remarkable. However, the point of the window, the interior's projection, contains a pipe column. Spanning across this hidden support is a beam that catches the long beams near the edge of the roof beyond their midpoints. The cantilever is the

Figure 4.8. Edward E. Boynton House, Rochester, New York.
(Photograph by John Waters)

Figure 4.9. Edward E. Boynton House. Dining room.
(Photograph by John Waters)

Figure 4.10. Edward E. Boynton House. Dining room.
(Photograph by John Waters)

Figure 4.11. Frederick C. Robie House, Chicago.
(Photograph by Sidney K. Robinson)

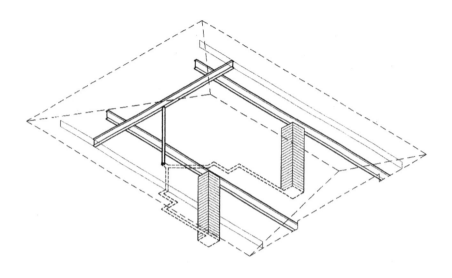

Figure 4.12. Frederick C. Robie House, Chicago. Cantilever structure.
(Drawing by Patrick Kinsfather)

real mechanism that destroys the box. The double cantilever expands the building's boundary and the plasticity of the perimeter, breaking out of the containment characteristic of column and beam structure. The angled glass point at the end of the orthogonal living room projects under the cantilevered roof whose soaring structure depends on the point support hidden in the very element that expands the interior space. Any attempt to decide which came first, the structure or the definition of space, is dismissed by the crossover diagram in this narrative that proposes how each can be seen from the perspective of the other; space led the structure and structure led the space.

The column and beam at the point of the Robie House living room form a T, a beam balanced at its midpoint, the simplest diagram of a cantilever (fig. 4.12). A very early example of this "T" cantilever is

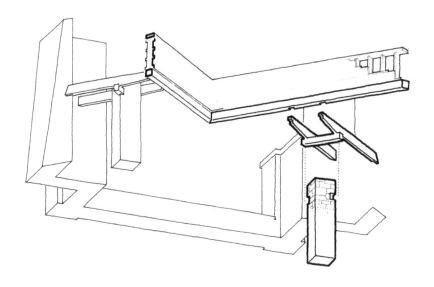

Figure 4.13. Hillside Home School, Spring Green, Wisconsin. Assembly room detail. (Drawing by Patrick Kinsfather)

found in the 1903 Hillside School assembly room (figs. 4.13, 4.14, 4.15). In fact the diagonally rotated balcony in this centralized room is largely structurally supported and visually primarily supported by a three step "T" cantilever system. The balcony fronts with their inner layers of diagonal boards are supported at their midpoints by beams extending out from the stone piers at the room's corners. The four-square stability of the surrounding building sets up the animating contrast of structures and floating corner. The beams supporting the middles of the balconies are cantilevered on short wooden members sticking out of the sides of the piers. This Calder-like sequence of cantilevers creates a floating ambiguity of how the rotated balcony is supported. By rotating the balcony, Wright suspends its corners in midair. This breaks the box of orthogonal corner support. The corners, usually the most significant point of support, are, instead, cantilevered from their beams' midpoints. The significance of this

Figure 4.14. Hillside Home School. Assembly room. Balcony supported at its center. (Drawing by John H. Waters)

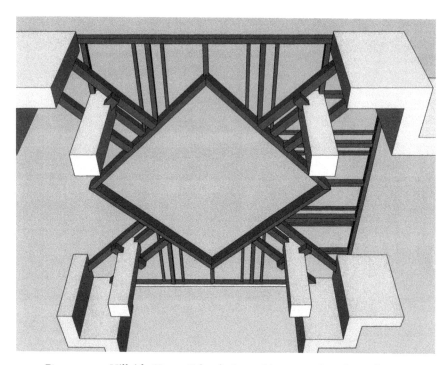

Figure 4.15. Hillside Home School. Assembly room. Set of cantilevers supporting the balcony. (Drawing by John H. Waters)

Figure 4.16. Hillside Home School. Assembly room.
(Photograph by Sidney K. Robinson)

structure is made evident when one considers what the room would look like if, rather than being rotated, the balcony had simply spanned from corner stone pier to stone pier (fig. 4.16). The familiar orthogonal pattern would make a static, clearly outlined room. For some this certainty is reassuring, for Wright it was dead.

The complex boundary creating an interior spatial sequence where one space leads in anticipation of the next space is another mark of Wright's architecture. It's a little like a film sequence when the sound of the next scene is heard before the next scene appears. A compelling example is found in the stair in Fallingwater. When spaces lead, when they set up anticipations of where one is headed next, the distinction of one space and the next is blurred. In this case the stair is not simply a passage. It would be hard to say when the boundary of one location was clearly crossed. Of course, the descent reenacts the crossing over of spatial conditions looking down (fig. 4.17).

Figure 4.17. Liliane S. and Edgar J. Kaufmann Sr. House (Fallingwater),
Mill Run, Pennsylvania. Stair. (Photograph by Christopher Little,
courtesy the Western Pennsylvania Conservancy)

CROSSING BOUNDARIES WITH FRANK LLOYD WRIGHT

A common pattern in the Oak Park Studio residential designs was a single volume containing both living room and dining room, as in the Cheney, Parton, Wescott, and Walser Houses, as well as many others. The space may be continuous, but the distinguishing separation is achieved by wood trim, free-standing cabinets, and associated members spanning below the ceiling. In terms of merging functions, the striking presence of the dining area in the Glasner House (1905) next to the living room fireplace is a very early dispensing of even modified separations between living and dining. This example clearly presages the Usonian simplifications, or rather the maximal merging of different functional and spatial characteristics. The Robie House is a highly developed example of continuous space and articulated distinctions as mentioned above.[218]

In planning terms, the familiar overlap of the living room and dining room volumes of the Charles Ross Cottage (1902) displays the complex boundary between the two spaces that are individual at their extremities but continuous at the overlap. You know where you are at their perimeters but cannot be sure when moving or looking at their proximity. The "open plan" is another way to describe how spaces, both for functional and perceptual reasons, are continuous. The "tartan grid," so named in Richard MacCormac's essay, is a pattern with historical roots as mentioned above. The historical basilical plan and section, a wide and high central space bordered by narrow, low spaces, can be expanded as a grid that can be called a tartan grid: narrow-wide-narrow repeated. When one approaches the wide space, the nave, from the narrow zone, the side aisle, there is a distinct transition from narrow and low to wide and high. Extending this pattern into a field became a major conventional tool for laying out plans. It is a significant example of Wright taking what is a convention of long standing in architectural history and reinterpreting it for his own use. When Wright is laying out plans with this grid, he uses it for two main reasons: it prepares the experience of arrival, and it is very useful for functional reasons. The common reference is to "compression/ release" arrival experience as if that is some uniquely Wrightian architectural discovery. In exterior settings, it is simply walking under a gate; the Romans set up that sequence all over Rome. When Wright added his buildings to his aunts' Hillside Home School in 1903, he located two parts of the program on either side of the original entrance drive. To get from one building to the other he spanned over the drive with an enclosed bridge. As you entered the School compound, you went under the bridge and arrived at the open space of the campus. In functional terms, a clear example is the dining room of the Heller House. The square space for the table is framed by two narrow spaces, one for cabinetry and one serving the entrance from the kitchen; "servant and served" spaces, in other terms. The "side aisle" spaces are for service, entry, and preparation. The dining room, for example, in the Fricke House is similarly laid out.

The complex boundary is significant from the outside in and from the inside out. A marvelous example of the latter is the built-in seat at the breakfast alcove end of the Thomas House dining room. The part of the house projecting the most at the sidewalk perimeter and at the height of not quite a second story is located at the thick transition zone between inside and out. Surrounded by windows, this space permits a view across the street, but more significantly up and down the street and under a major roof cantilever. Sitting at that alcove you have left the enclosure of the house and entered into the world outside. The entrance sequence at the Thomas House is also notable as one passes between two walls of leaded glass. This zone of color and light is not outside nor inside but an intermediate zone that sets off both conditions going either in or out.

Wright explored ways to expand the transition zone in two houses separated by three decades: the Meyer May House of 1908 and the Willey House of 1933. In both instances a glazed ceiling meeting a glazed wall creates a place that complexly embraces inside and out. In the Meyer May House, leaded lay lights illuminate a lower perimeter zone at the garden edge of the living room, whose wall is a row of large windows aligned with the glass ceiling (fig. 4.18). Looking from the living room proper, the

Figure 4.18. Meyer May House, Grand Rapids, Michigan. Lay lights. (Photograph courtesy Steelcase, Inc.)

light from above and from the wall anticipates an outdoor condition while being inside. The Willey House extends this complexity because the glazed wall can actually be crossed through a row of French doors (fig. 4.19). One reaches this amazing zone from a living room whose ceiling slopes from a high point at the massive brick fireplace opposite the doors down to a lower flat ceiling coming from the entrance door (fig. 4.20). The transition from the major slope to the flat ceiling is made by a sharper slope that connects the flat ceiling and the major ceiling. This connecting plane, effecting a significant volumetric transition, spans across the whole width of the living room (fig. 4.21). Although there is a steel beam supporting that span now, Wright's initial proposal was an example of his thinking how folded planes could contribute to structure as well as

Figure 4.19. Nancy and Malcolm E. Willey House, Minneapolis, Minnesota.
(Photograph by Sidney K. Robinson)

Figure 4.20. Nancy and Malcolm E. Willey House.
(Photograph by Sidney K. Robinson)

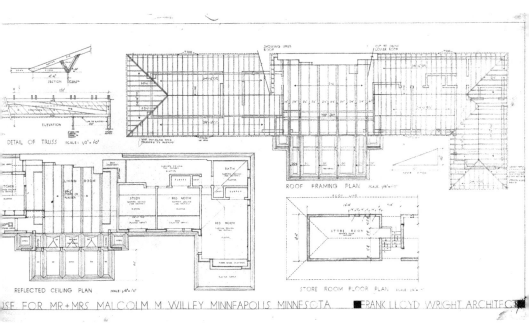

DETAIL OF TRUSS SCALE: 1/2"=1'0"

ELEVATION

ROOF FRAMING PLAN SCALE 1/4"=1'0"

LIVING ROOM

STUDY   BED ROOM

BATH

BED ROOM

STORE ROOM

REFLECTED CEILING PLAN   SCALE 1/4"=1'0"

STORE ROOM FLOOR PLAN SCALE 1/4"=1'0"

USE FOR MR+MRS MALCOLM M WILLEY MINNEAPOLIS MINNESOTA   FRANK LLOYD WRIGHT ARCHITECT

Figure 4.21. Nancy and Malcolm E. Willey House.
The Frank Lloyd Wright Foundation Archives (The Museum of Modern Art |
Avery Architectural & Fine Arts Library, Columbia University, New York)

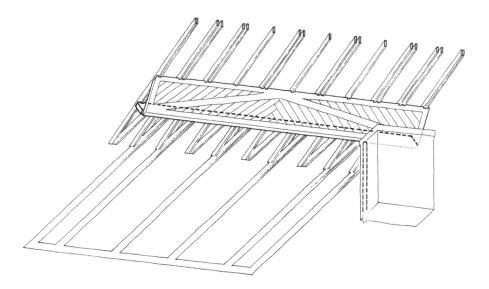

Figure 4.22. Nancy and Malcolm E. Willey House.
(Drawing by Patrick Kinsfather)

spatial definition. The angle of the sharper sloped plane became one side of a triangular truss-like tube made of wood members covered by the plaster of the ceiling. Wood sheathing enclosed diagonal 2″ x 8″s spanning the 12′2″ from the bearing points on 2″ steel pipes at the ends (fig. 4.22). This proposal accomplished two things: it avoided a heavy steel member Wright often rejected as unnecessary in a residence, and it demonstrated how form had both spatial and structural roles. The continuity of the ceiling planes from high to transition to flat is emphasized by the wood stripping whose pattern is generated by the divisions of the French doors and continue up the steep transition slope all the way to the opposite brick fireplace wall. Embedding structure into the transition fold is classic Wright, constructing continuity by combining the articulation of form and structure. Of course, a steel beam was substituted! Wright's preference to avoid steel beams and his desire to unite structure with space formation would have produced a unique solution. This combination of space formation and structure also appears in the 1930s expansion of the Taliesin living room window-wall where sloped roof, horizontal soffit, and the vertical plane connecting ceiling to soffit make a similar triangular structural tube whose diagonal truss members are hidden under the plaster.

The complex boundary at the Willey House living room garden wall reaches an amazing climax when the glazed doors are met by the glazed ceiling. Rather than the flat, leaded lay lights of the May House, the Willey glazed ceiling is accomplished by sloped, tentlike panes (fig. 4.23). The openings in the ceiling continue the open trellis extending outside from the doors. All of these formal moves intensify the complexity of the boundary between inside and out. But there is more, of course. The brick terrace that continues the interior brick flooring takes an angular turn at 30 degrees right under the inner edge of the skylights. The continuity of overlap between interior and exterior is emphasized by this geometric turn. The continuous brick paving potentially creates a way for water to slide under the door frames. The current solution is a row of bricks specially molded with a slight hump to engage the flashing at the

Figure 4.23. Nancy and Malcolm E. Willey House.
(Photograph by Sidney K. Robinson)

bottom of the doors. The angles introduced by the angled terrace appear in the exquisite bevels framing the doors and the skylights. It is a further exercise of a complex boundary that actually starts at the opposite wall and continues to the end of the cantilevered trellis. The beveled members around the skylights match the frame at the top of the doors and continue outside into the profile of the trellis members. The energized displacement introduced by the angular form is most evident in the way the center line of the skylight framing bevel does not connect with the center line of the door frames. This slight offset contributes to the boundary complexity that would not occur with a simple, direct parallelism. The Willey House, from fireplace to trellis, is a lesson on boundary crossing from the large scale of the whole room to the small details of door frames. Structure, spatial configuration, and complex boundary are at a level that seals the proposition of Wright's comprehensive way of making buildings.

The folded plane that appears in the Willey House as a structural tube is just one further example of the second structural means Wright uses to construct the complex boundaries being examined here. The cantilever is somehow a more obvious method. The folded plane is less obvious. As was introduced in the first chapter, the goal of making architecture not of pieces, but of continuities lies at the heart of Wright's architecture.

Unity Temple is a significant stage in his exploration of how form and structure can be unified. The final form for the interior of Unity Temple is a graphic lesson signifying how the orthogonal planes of traditional construction can be made continuous. When Wright proposes that this building is an important initial step in his search for a modern architecture, he leads with its example as a concrete monolith. According to the magnificent perspective of Marion Mahony, its forms, like those of the Larkin Building, its obvious precedent in Wright's work, are initially represented in brick. Stone coping and bases maintain the conventions of masonry construction. When cost became an issue and concrete was proposed, Wright continued with that convention by proposing that the walls, but not the coping or bases, should have a red granite aggregate to preserve the distinction of the traditional formal elements. Of course that tedious application of concrete with two kinds of aggregate was rejected for probably costing even more. Only then did the significance of the continuity of the concrete material appear as an architectural goal. Extending the potentials of that newly recognized goal of continuity, the interior ornament evolved as was illustrated in the Introduction (figs. 4–6). The wood stripping folding around structural corners diagrammed continuity whose implications were yet to be fully explored. When the plan and section of Unity Temple is placed in the context of architectural traditions, it clearly follows precedents set centuries ago. For a religious, or even just an important community building, Unity Temple is an example based on the basilica model going back at least to Rome. A major central space, high and wide, is surrounded by lower, narrower spaces—think Gothic cathedrals' nave and side-aisles. A centralized example of the plan, octagonal here, and section is found in San Vitale, the Byzantine basilica (527–547) in Ravenna, Italy. The form of Unity Temple is updated tradition; its ornament is groundbreaking departure.

The wood stripping that first appeared to outline constructional members of Unity Temple now folds around corners uniting the planes, or as occurs at the top of the four corner piers, obscures those members by overrunning their boundaries with the wood stripping pattern. The concrete material of Unity Temple is also the forerunner of Wright's later embracing of reinforced concrete as plane rather than mass. The Guggenheim Museum in New York is basically Unity Temple in the round: two parts linked, the larger volume with balconies lighted from above. The plasticity of Unity Temple's square is completely replaced by the continuity of the curve. To say that the Guggenheim is not plastic seems counterintuitive except when one refers back to the original characteristic of projections and recesses which produce corners. Wright's structural plane ideal was pushed beyond 1940s calculations when he proposed the Guggenheim's spiral plane folded up as wall at the exterior and as railing

Figure 4.24. Midway Gardens, Chicago. South wall of Tavern Room. (Photograph by Henry Fuermann, courtesy the Eric O'Malley Collection/OA+D Archives)

CROSSING BOUNDARIES WITH FRANK LLOYD WRIGHT

on the interior. The image Wright used to describe this self-supporting continuity was a spring. The disappointment that necessitated vertical fins to support the ramp was somewhat mitigated by having those fins' structural function virtually disappear by the time they met the ground. When the demonstration of structure was a primary goal for architecture, what was seen as Wright's transgression was simply a misunderstanding of what his goal was. The formal continuity of planes challenged the current structural analysis of continuous structure as Wright learned from Beggs, the Princeton engineer. The formal exploration of folded planes, initially just patterns bending over changes in plane, occurs in the Oak Park Studio work that exploited the wood stripping that wraps horizontally around wall projections and recesses, and vertically as it united the tops of walls with ceilings. This graphic expression anticipates the potential of actually constructing continuity. This intermediate stage of exploration is partial; it suggests continuity by the clever manipulation of parts, not actually merging them; that comes later with reinforced concrete.

Bending patterns around corners, whether wood strips or paint colors, emphasizes the continuity of surfaces for both aesthetic and structurally suggestive purposes. The patterns of the amazing murals in the smoking bar of the Midway Gardens continued beyond the recessed panel framing them by bending over the recess (fig. 4.24). This continuity has a singular effect. Parts that are volumetrically separate are drawn together: ceilings and walls, ceiling planes, ceilings and exterior soffits. Wright's folded planes had to be distinguished from the planar architecture of the European modernists: "But most new 'modernistic' houses manage to look as though cut from cardboard with scissors, the sheets of cardboard folded or bent in rectangles with an occasional curved cardboard surface added to get relief."[219] Those folded planes were simply compositions; Wright knew how the fold was not just an aesthetic element, it could also have structural significance as vital contributions to plasticity and continuity. In the early buildings, constructed of wood with masonry elements, the wood walls are 2″ x 4″ studs with diagonal laths covered with plaster. The whole assembly acquires a degree of unification that approaches a single, structural plane. There are times in the original Taliesin where what appears to simply be a plastered wall is, to some degree, acting as a deep, planar beam carrying an opening or part of a cantilever.

In the camp at Chandler, Arizona, Wright enclosed Ocatillo (1928) with a board and batten wood wall that he stiffened for lateral strength with a series of 30 by 60-degree angled folds reinforced at points with triangular tubes acting as posts (fig. 4.25). This angular geometry appears in the plan arrangement of the various small structures and in their sections as well. The formal and structural consequences of this angled geometry extend the potentials of continuity and plasticity. The irregular, geometrically wandering wall at Ocatillo encloses the top of the hill as it moves from building walls to freestanding garden walls. This 30/60 geometry, more flexible in adjustment to site conditions, is later cited as more convenient for human movement when it is used to lay out building plans in the hexagonal units explored in the Hanna House in Palo Alto. The 90-degree folds in Wright's previous buildings emphasized the plasticity of the projections and recesses of corners, while the 30/60 geometry approached the goal of continuity by minimizing the abrupt planar changes of orthogonality. When circular forms appear, continuity achieves dominance at the expense of plasticity. The corners characteristic of most constructional materials disappear in the continuity of the curved forms of poured concrete.

The appearance in 1928 of the 30/60 geometry, the "reflex" geometry, signals a major increase in Wright's set of geometries. The structural potential of this geometry was explored immediately in the proposals for the major 1932 proposed expansion of the Hillside Home School for the Allied Arts, which set in motion the forms for the Taliesin West buildings. The symmetrical hipped roof geometry of Prairie School days was replaced by a single slope in the 30/60 angular mode, as at Ocatillo, whose slopes were to be supported by a number of triangular

Figure 4.25. Ocatillo Desert Camp, Chandler, Arizona.
(Photograph by George Kastner, Courtesy of Brian Spencer, Architect)

struts and three-dimensional trusses. Geometry again supports ornament, spatial composition, and structure.

Wright goes on to achieve a more viable planar structure with the solid, layered walls of the Usonian model. The three layers of wood, screwed tightly together, support a roof structure whose unconventional joists are built up of two-by-fours stacked three deep. The ends of each of these boards step back at the edge to further articulate the cantilever boundary. The structural plane of the wall, because it is intentionally thin, requires lateral bracing. Here is where the genius comes in. The way to stabilize a thin, continuous wall, as Jefferson shows in the single wythe brick walls at the University of Virginia, is to add depth through departing from straight, linear path by bending the wall in and out. The

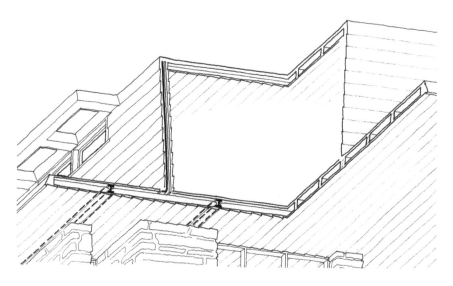

Figure 4.26. John Clarence Pew House, Shorewood Hills, Wisconsin.
(Drawing by Patrick Kinsfather)

Figure 4.27. John C. Pew House.
(Photograph by Sidney K. Robinson)

CROSSING BOUNDARIES WITH FRANK LLOYD WRIGHT

wall becomes thicker, not by more material, but by geometric movement. In the Usonian walls, Wright folds them and makes corners which—surprise, surprise—create a complex boundary that expands the zone of enclosure between inside and out. Again, form and structure are one.

In the Pew House (1938) this structural reading of the thin wood wall is made explicit by Wes Peters's oral history of his construction of the house (figs. 4.26, 4.27). William Wesley Peters signed on with Wright in 1932 after studying at MIT; his appreciation of structure facilitated Wright's evolution of structural experimentation. The bedrooms were to cantilever over the carport. Peters expressed concern that the steel beams of the cantilever structure were not enough to carry the bedrooms above. Following Wright's conception of planar structure, planes acting as deep beams: "We discussed how are we going to tie the upper bedrooms in to make it part of the cantilever. So we finally got very heavy grade sheet metal, something like 10 or 12 gauge sheet metal...and put in [between the '3/4 in. plywood core with overlapping board-and batten effects on both sides of the wall'] and turned [the steel sheets] into a flange at right angles to the vertical at the bottom... and bolted to all the rafters and wood beams and the steel and wood flitch plates that carried the cantilever. So this made the whole upper part, the bedroom part, organically a part of the structure below, sharing the cantilever."[220] He says explicitly that, knowing that the wood wall planes should be examples of structure and form together, he adds to their structural capacity by layering into the wood layers a sheet of heavy gage sheet metal. This is the clearest testimony of Wright's way of thinking of form and structure simultaneously. When Peters reinforced the wood wall he, in effect, expanded the familiar flitch-plate beam into a structural plane replacing linear members with structure as enclosure. The original proposal for the Pope-Leighey House reinforced the wall spanning the dining alcove with a similar layer of sheet metal. Without the advantage of Wes Peters's insight, a steel beam was used instead. The reinforced planar structure of the Pew House is

Figure 4.28. Herbert and Katherine Jacobs House, Madison, Wisconsin. (Photograph by Pedro Guerrero, courtesy Dixie Legler)

not knowable from the drawings and certainly not by direct inspection. So what is the point? Like cantilevers crossing over blank walls with no obvious shading function, the ideal of form, proposed here as having its basis from the perspective of ornament, has an intellectual function.

The layered wood wall construction of the first Jacobs House, and subsequent Usonian houses, in addition to their structural function, contributed to the weaving metaphor by means of their board-and-batten pattern (fig. 4.28). The wide pine boards were separated by narrow redwood strips slightly recessed. The traditional board-and-batten construction was a way to cover the joints between the major boards. That method makes sense when employed in a vertical orientation. Water drains down along the joints. When Wright turns the boards horizontally, he contradicts that logic; now the water is flowing across the joints. However, the resulting horizontal continuity of the structural plane can fold back and forth to achieve stability and plasticity. It also brings in the weaving metaphor to the structural, volumetric, and complex boundary synthesisin Wright's architecture.

A parallel metaphor for construction of planar structures is the weaving or fabric model seen in the California textile block houses. Taking the weaving model to an extreme, Wright constructs walls of masonry units interlaced with steel rods. In a way it is a reinforced concrete wall with large, regular aggregate. This construction as a wall is not immediately transferable to spanning or cantilevering. In these examples Wright explores the tradition of wall architecture appropriate for the Southwest and California sites. The cantilever often appears in the textile block houses as concrete blocks supported by wood beams or by reinforced concrete members. The Usonian Automatic houses of the 1950s used larger blocks and poured concrete slabs to support cantilevers, sometimes of dramatic extent as in the Kalil House (1955). The weaving metaphor breaks down as do the walls when water corrodes the steel rods tying the blocks together.

Taliesin West's desert masonry becomes structural masses supporting spanning elements. Cantilevers are difficult here too. For all Wright's condemnation of the post-and-beam structural system, when faced with spanning the drafting rooms of both Taliesin and Taliesin West, he camouflaged the spanning element. At Taliesin the truss has extra members called out with red edges that suggest cantilevering from the "posts" that are not simple vertical elements, but triangular forms touching down with beautiful cast metal toes. At Taliesin West, the beams are tilted and meet their "posts" by two right-angled turns that hang off the wall or pier. The one building that brought the desert masonry and planar wood wall together was the Pauson House (1939), whose desert concrete masses were linked by layered wood walls of lapped boards rather than the flat board-and-batten Usonian model. It is curious that Wright did not pursue this combination, intriguing as it seems; maybe because it crossed too many metaphors!

Another brief exploration of the structural plane was sketched out in the 1937–38 All Steel Houses. Sheet metal channels 9" wide and 7/8" or 2" deep are connected side by side to function as self-supporting planes: walls, floors, and roofs, in two or three layers as the spans required. As Wright described them: "Sheet Metal Structures for dwellings—Unit System—One section used throughout—interpenetrated with windows and doors—Sheet Metal Sections perforated for glass insertions for windows."[221] This extension of the woven plane metaphor into horizontal and vertical striated surfaces forming a steel membrane produced volumes very like the concrete block walls of the textile houses. However, the steel planes provided the cantilevers that the bearing masonry block construction did not. The geometric mesh of the weaving metaphor exactly describes the construction and appearance of these basically undeveloped schemes.

Reinforced concrete does it all; it is both planar structure and space forming at a scale only dreamed of in wood. The freedom to span and support, fold and return that reinforced concrete supplies is wonderful. When one thinks of the concrete of Fallingwater, the balconies, the cantilevers of light-colored concrete almost don't read as structure. Of course, there are significant beams supporting the whole stack of terraces, but the predominant reading is planes floating. Floating is the point. One of the ways to make a complex boundary is to avoid making the gravity-resisting load paths clear. Starting back with the Hillside Home School assembly room with its rotated mezzanine, making it not obvious what is holding up and what is doing the holding, distracts from a clear reading of where the boundaries of the spaces actually are. Post-and-beam structure often sets up boundaries of both exterior and interior volumes. Wright also uses a trick not unknown to architects generally of suspending the second floor over a wide first floor room from rods coming from the second floor connecting to roof trusses. The width of the Bradley living room is halved by a beam supported by rods encased in the second-floor closets. Stepping into the Bradley living room, all one registers is how spacious it is. This effect does not stimulate questioning just how that result was achieved. The steel rods can be in tension as well as suspension. In the Robert Llewellyn Wright House, the cantilevered balcony off the master bedroom projects from the narrow dimension at the end of the lens-shaped plan. What holds this balcony up is a rod at the end of the cantilevered steel beam with virtually no back span that is anchored into the foundation. Such deception has led some to characterize some of Wright's structures as "aerial foundations;" to get to the ground you first have to follow the load path up, then over, and finally down to the ground. Linear structure sets up predicable rhythms that establish limits as gravity is clearly being directed. The floating, folded plane delineates no such clear boundary. A stunning example of this approach is the Pfeiffer Chapel (1938) at Florida Southern College. The tower hovers over the assembly by magic. What holds up this reflector of light is uncertain, hard to follow, uplifting rather than weighing down. "Natural" light, meaning coming in from the outside, is the great boundary crosser. The way it gets into the chapel, the uncertainty of support, makes the whole top of the assembly space a crossover boundary that connects the congregation with the light of the spirit. It is a magnificent demonstration of Wright's ability to direct attention from one place or condition across the expanded reality of boundary to another place.

Probably the most recognized feature of Wright's architecture are the cantilevers that soar beyond the perimeter boundaries of the buildings. They may have an obvious shading or sheltering function: over windows, covering entrances or carports, for example. It is surprising

Figure 4.29. Pope-Leighey House, Alexandria, Virginia.
Exterior photo showing bedroom end. (Photograph by Lincoln Barbour,
courtesy National Trust for Historic Preservation)

when they project above a blank wall. At the bedroom end of the Affleck House in Michigan, a trellis cantilever projects over a blank brick wall. Further boundary crossing is achieved by a brick-walled planter projected under the cantilever. These two extensions beyond the enclosure cannot be explained except as formal means to expand the boundary of the house. These terminals of the artifact are not readily seen when approaching the house. You have to take in the whole construction to find them. This fact is the most convincing evidence that form has a function beyond performance or instrumentality. Cantilevers can be primarily factors in the complex boundary, the continuity/plasticity function that is also what Wright's architecture is about. In the Brown and Fuller Houses, for example, a large cantilever projects over the porch. The structure that supports this cantilever is one that Wright uses repeatedly. The rule of thumb for designing a cantilever is that the back end of the members

Figure 4.30. Pope-Leighey House, Alexandria, Virginia.
Exterior photo showing living room end. (Photograph by Lincoln Barbour,
courtesy National Trust for Historic Preservation)

are two thirds the length of the beam. This, of course, is based on the member acting by itself. In the Brown and Fuller Houses and, for another example, the balcony off the Loggia at Taliesin, there is virtually no back span because that short, conventionally inadequate span is loaded by weight that counteracts the extension of the cantilever itself. At Taliesin this load is applied by masonry piers in the room above, functioning simultaneously as space definer and active structural element. This backloading is not something Wright invented but is a very useful technique to make it difficult to read how the cantilever is supported. In the Brown House, the back span load is provided by the second-story wall and the roof loads that counteract the extended porch roof.

The question, "What is the cantilever for," arises when there is no obvious sheltering function. An example is the McCartney House, where a large, pointed cantilever extends over what is basically a blank, brick wall of a closet. In the flat-roofed Usonian houses, roof cantilevers perforated as trellises project beyond the wood or masonry walls where there is no shading or sheltering function. Clear examples of how a roof cantilever is not determined by the condition of the wall underneath it are the two ends of the L-shaped Pope-Leighey House (figs. 4.29, 4.30). At the bedroom end, the projecting trellis cantilever is over windows with the same spacing as the trellis. At the living room end, the story and a half wood wall is topped by a band of perforated boards. Several feet of cantilever of beams projects over the wall. The cantilever is not noticeable from the inside, only from the outside; that must be where it contributes to a complex boundary. These two examples—there are more, of course—demonstrate how a complex boundary determines the form of the building. Such projections serve the formal function of expanding the depth of the perimeter beyond an abrupt termination. Imagining the Pope-Leighey House without those cantilevers explains it all. Something would be missing. It is interesting that one does not have to be an architect concerned with how a building looks to see that something is wrong. Of further significance is that this view of the building is not seen from the common approach to the house. You have to walk around the house to see these cantilevers. And yet without them, something is missing.

The Pope-Leighey house, in addition to displaying the cantilever, also demonstrates how thin walls can be folded to serve both as structure and space definer. The Usonian three-layered wood wall without conventional studs had to prove its structural capabilities when a section of the Pope-Leighey house was loaded up with bags of cement. In addition to the wall's direct bearing capacity, its structural stability depended on the corners made by its bends at the ends of both the living and bedroom wings. In the living room, the walls folding at the dining alcove with its cantilevering roof plane and the projection of the row of French doors opposite stabilize long, high wall planes. At the bedroom end, a fold in the wall terminates the hall to provide an entry into the bedroom, and the wall and window plane at the end of the room bends back to expose a brick planter while the roof's cantilever extends the ceiling plane.

When structure and enclosure are combined, deflecting a clear reading of how loads are being supported, the need to stabilize thin walls results in folds that create the plasticity crossing the boundaries between rooms and between inside and outside. As Gordon Chadwick, the Taliesin Fellow who oversaw construction of the Pope-Leighey house reported: "Mr. Wright thought of these walls as screens . . . [he]often spoke of 'plasticity' and I suspect this principle is involved here."[222] It should be recalled that Wright referred to the concrete walls of Unity Temple as "screens" thirty years before. The continuity of principle is obvious!

These compositions of overlapping planes: wall, window, masonry, ceiling and cantilever at the ends of the building, a kind of telescoping extension from inside to outside, create complex boundaries. Cantilever and structural plane are the primary architectural means Wright crosses over the boundary of the building's interior and exterior volumes. Both of these features can be seen as having their roots in the categories of continuity and plasticity carried over from ornament. The initial Usonian houses are so important because they combine so many of Wright's principles: the art of architecture available in American citizens in their residences, a system of design and building, new materials and technologies, the simultaneity of fluid structure and spatial definition, and most significantly here, as demonstrations of how ornament led to architecture.

CONCLUSION

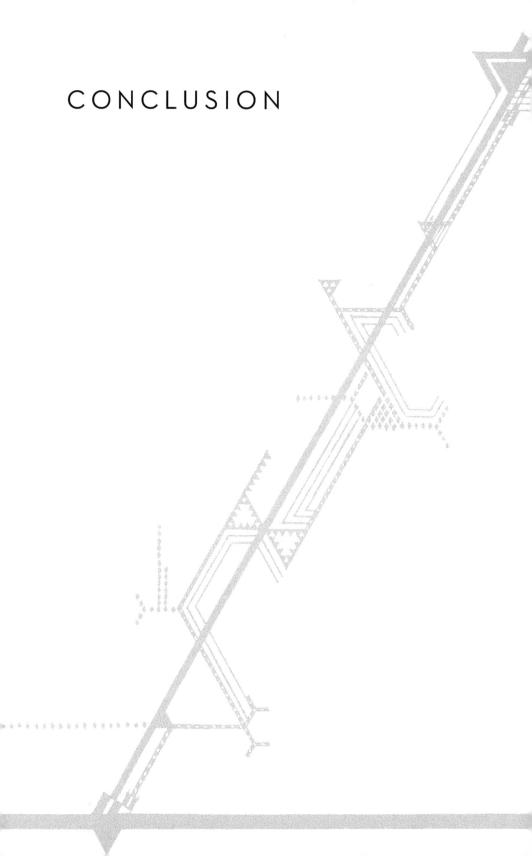

F rank Lloyd Wright's habit of expanding the dimension where inside and outside cross over encourages movement and active visual inspection. Crossing boundaries creates architecture that invites active engagement, not passive regard. Wright developed this condition of complex interaction in part because he interpreted Louis Sullivan's ornament, not as design, but as the conceptual principle of continuity and plasticity. The crossover pattern leads to making buildings, but it originated in the abstract potentials Wright saw in ornament. Materials (ornament) led to abstraction (conceptions) led back to materials (architecture), tracking his powerful capacity for interpretation not imitation. He did not make buildings by imitating Sullivan's ornament; he interpreted its conceptual implications, its potential to lead to architecture through radical abstraction.

The process of abstracting from ornament to structure led Wright to two important means to construct his architecture: the cantilever and planar structure. Using these two means, he was able to achieve the complex boundaries that reach out and draw in along a building's perimeter and the composition of interior spaces. Each of these constructional examples contributes to continuity by linking inside to outside and to plasticity by activating buildings' enclosures with projections and recessions at their edges. This combination of linking and separating is also the major characteristic of Wright's interiors that create "space" that is articulated by its complex boundaries.

This exploration of a pattern that Frank Lloyd Wright used to design and to think has revealed the power and the challenge of expanding the edges of buildings and thoughts. It can be unsettling to some because it creates uncertainty regarding the location of limits and boundaries, but when Wright expands intersections by projecting and receding across a boundary, it increases the range of both function and form. When Wright examined architecture using words, he kept proposing and then critiquing his conceptions of architectural goals and means. When he designed buildings, he expanded the interface between inside and out to enhance the architectural relationship with human activity and environmental conditions. In both cases a conceptual and spatial thickness made for artifacts that activated alternative interpretations. Constant exploration is the way to avoid getting stuck or becoming comfortable on one side of the boundary or the other.

The two words Wright repeatedly used to characterize his architecture—the *continuity* and *plasticity* he heard about and observed in Louis Sullivan's ornament—were the conceptual conveyances that carried him across the boundary between ornament and architecture, but they eventually made the journey increasingly challenging. From the outset of his career, he sought out continuity as the characteristic that would distinguish his architecture from the historical conventions of structure, construction, and formal composition. At the same time, however, he embraced the nature of materials, which inherently meant designing with joints. Continuity strived to erase joints; the nature of materials, plasticity, reveled in them. That is one reason the weaving metaphor Wright uses for his architecture is so apposite; its "joints" of weft and warp create an articulated continuity.

When, in 1927, Wright imagined that the potential forms for concrete "may take the shapes characteristic of drifted snow or sand," his vision eliminates the effort required to work with a palette of materials and the joints they required.[223] (These striking images of concrete's form may have been prompted by the visit to Taliesin in 1924 by Erich Mendelsohn, who had just completed the Einstein Tower outside Berlin in an Expressionist, "organic" form, displaying the fluid character of poured concrete, but actually executed in stucco-covered brick.) The granular scale of the continuous surfaces of snow or sand no longer requires the assembly of parts. One may wonder if the result finally escapes architecture "in the grand old sense of structural tradition," as Wright described it in the 1901 "Art and Craft of the Machine." Or do such images instead anticipate a whole new digital world he tentatively predicted but did not pursue as he continued to use the geometry constructed by the instruments on his drafting board? Wright, given the computer capabilities that, say, Frank Gehry has today, may have found an answer. But only if the nature of materials is simply set aside as an important constituent of Wright's architecture. Trying to preserve the contribution of both these categories, working across the boundary that distinguishes continuity from plasticity, may have prevented realizing the literal continuity of form seen in sand and snow. Constructing continuity by assembling materials made the intention to achieve continuity accessible and instructive. When Wright embraced the continuity of concrete, he questioned his commitment to the inherent plasticity, the projections and recesses of the different formal, textural, chromatic, and structural nature of materials in favor of concrete's continuity. One could observe that the plaster surfaces of the Oak Park houses create a kind of material continuity, but this liquid material was always stopped at trim and structural members. Fallingwater may be so compelling not just because of its dramatic rhyming of its setting, but because it combines the continuity of concrete with the plasticity of the masonry; both goals are powerfully met.

The Rose Pauson house (1938-41, destroyed 1943) is a surprising parallel to Fallingwater's combination of continuity and plasticity. The folds in the thin, lapped wood walls of the Pauson house create continuity like the concrete planes in Fallingwater, and those wood walls project from masonry whose stunning plasticity of desert concrete recalls the sandstone of Fallingwater. I would venture to say that these two buildings embody the most successful combination of continuity and plasticity in Wright's work.

Giving up the creative tension in trying to construct continuity and plasticity, a tension inherent from the beginning when Wright set out the principles of his architecture, may have finally been resolved by no longer working at their interface, by subsiding into repose, also one of Wright's earliest architectural goals. Repose excludes the tension between continuity and plasticity. Wright's "organic architecture," encompassing both the resolution, the stasis of Unity Temple and the evolution, the changes of Taliesin required constant negotiation of the difference between continuity and plasticity. That effort took energy to think and construct. The hobbit-like busy-ness that some people see in Wright's architecture can be an invitation to travel the crossing path, while others may want to arrive not to explore. And maybe in Wright's later years, he too may have tired of exploring and simply wanted to arrive.

Crossing boundaries with Frank Lloyd Wright has led us to see a pattern of thought, expression, and design that results in a nuanced understanding of material construction, but more importantly to see ways of understanding and interacting with the world at large by avoiding simple opposition. The present examination set out not to prove, but to observe. Others may see different patterns. I hope you can find further examples of the crossover pattern I have been tracing. It may contribute to other designs and thoughts without suggesting that Wright's specific formal means to produce complex boundaries is the only way. One consequence of following this proposition may be that architects can interpret Wright's contribution without mimicking it. That challenge applies to learning from any source, whether a group or an individual. Wright himself showed how this could be done when he learned from Louis Sullivan not by copying him, but by building on what he started. Would it be fair to say that Wright did not honor his Lieber Meister because he significantly departed from Sullivan's path? The way Wright interpreted Sullivan took off in directions Sullivan would never have taken but set up for others to follow.

The abstraction of pattern prepares for further work by looking for boundaries that have been crossed. It does not provide a set of forms but a way to proceed. The end point is not determined. I hope that Wright can be a mentor to future creators of artifacts and propositions that are not mirrors or echoes, but worthy descendants of Frank Lloyd Wright's achievements.

NOTES

INTRODUCTION

1. Frank Lloyd Wright, *An Autobiography* (New York: Duell, Sloan and Pearce, 1943), 4.

2. Wright, *An Autobiography*, 287.

3. Peter Blake, *The Master Builders* (New York: Alfred A. Knopf, 1961), 7.

4. Frank Lloyd Wright and Bruce Brooks Pfeiffer, *Frank Lloyd Wright Collected Writings, vol. 1, 1894–1931* (New York; [Scottsdale, AZ]: Rizzoli; Frank Lloyd Wright Foundation, 1992), 262.

5. Frank Lloyd Wright, *The Natural House* (New York: Horizon Press, 1954), 80.

6. Wright and Pfeiffer, *Frank Lloyd Wright Collected Writings*, 1:117.

7. Frank Lloyd Wright, *Genius and the Mobocracy* (New York: Duell, Sloan and Pearce, 1949), 64.

8. Wright, *An Autobiography*, 347–48.

9. Wright and Pfeiffer, *Frank Lloyd Wright Collected Writings, vol. 2, 1930–1932* (New York; [Scottsdale, AZ]: Rizzoli; Frank Lloyd Wright Foundation, 1992), 86.

10. Wright and Pfeiffer, *Frank Lloyd Wright Collected Writings*, 2:86–87.

11. Wright and Pfeiffer, *Frank Lloyd Wright Collected Writings*, 2:34.

12. Wright, *An Autobiography*, 181.

13. Wright and Pfeiffer, *Frank Lloyd Wright Collected Writings*, 1:59–60.

14. Wright and Pfeiffer, *Frank Lloyd Wright Collected Writings*, 2:87.

15. Le Corbusier and Frederick Etchells, *The City of To-morrow and Its Planning: With 215 Illustrations* (New York: Dover Publications, Inc, 1987), 5.

CHAPTER ONE

16. Louis H. Sullivan, *A System of Architectural Ornament According with a Philosophy of Man's Powers* (New York, Press of the American institute of Architects, Inc., 1924). The Auditorium Building, designed by the firm of Adler and Sullivan, is located in Chicago and owned by Roosevelt University. The Banqueting Hall is now called Ganz Hall and is used as a performance space.

17. Tim Samuelson, email to author, January 1, 2019. David Van Zanten, *Sullivan's City: The Meaning of Ornament for Louis Sullivan* (New York: W. W. Norton, 2000), 37.

18. Louis H. Sullivan and Lauren S. Weingarden, *Louis H. Sullivan: A System of Architectural Ornament* (New York: Rizzoli, in cooperation with the Art Institute of Chicago, 1990), 129.

19. Sullivan and Weingarden, *Louis H. Sullivan: A System of Architectural Ornament*, 133.

20. All of the following plates references are found in Sullivan and Weingarden, *Louis H. Sullivan: A System of Architectural Ornament*.

21. Louis H. Sullivan, "Ornament in Architecture," *The Engineering Magazine* (August 1892): 187–90.

22. Louis H. Sullivan, *Kindergarten Chats, and Other Writings* (New York: Dover Publications, 1979), 41.

23. Sullivan, *Kindergarten Chats*, 187.

24. Sullivan, *Kindergarten Chats*, 187–88.

25. Sullivan, *Kindergarten Chats*, 189.

26. Sullivan, *Kindergarten Chats*, 189.

27. John Holloway, "The Waste Land," *Encounter* XXXI, no. 2 (August 1968): 73–79.

28. Erich Auerbach, *Mimesis: The Representation of Reality in Western Literature* (Garden City, NY: Doubleday, 1953).

29. Holloway, "The Waste Land," 76.

30. Frank Lloyd Wright and Bruce Brooks Pfeiffer, *Frank Lloyd Wright Collected Writings, vol. 1, 1894–1931* (New York; [Scottsdale, AZ]: Rizzoli; Frank Lloyd Wright Foundation, 1992), 22.

31. Frank Lloyd Wright, "The Third Dimension," *Wendingen* VII, no. 4 (November 1925): 48–65.

32. Wright and Pfeiffer, *Frank Lloyd Wright Collected Writings*, 1:212.

33. Wright and Pfeiffer, *Frank Lloyd Wright Collected Writings*, 1:212.

34. Cornelis van de Ven, *Space in Architecture* (Amsterdam: Van Gorcum Assen, 1978), 231.

35. Wright and Pfeiffer, *Frank Lloyd Wright Collected Writings*, 1:178.

CHAPTER TWO

36. Debra Schafter, *The Order of Ornament, the Structure of Style: Theoretical Foundation of Modern Art and Architecture* (Cambridge: Cambridge University Press, 2003), 17.

37. E. H. Gombrich, *The Sense of Order: A Study in the Psychology of Decorative Art* (London: Phaidon Press, 1984), 53.

38. Schafter, *Order of Ornament*, 22.

39. Lada Hubatová-Vacková, *Silent Revolutions in Ornament: Studies in Applied Arts and Crafts from 1880–1930*, trans. Daniel Morgan, Kathleen Hayes (Prague: Academy of Arts, Architecture and Design, 2011), 204.

40. Hubatová-Vacková, *Silent Revolutions*, 49.

41. Philip Johnson, Alfred H. Barr, and Henry-Russell Hitchcock. *Modern Architecture: International Exhibition (Museum of Modern Art*: New York, 1932), 15.

42. Johnson, Barr, and Hitchcock, *Modern Architecture*, 34.

43. Schafter, *Order of Ornament*, 16.

44. Schafter, *Order of Ornament*, 16.

45. Hubatová-Vacková, *Silent Revolutions*, 22.

46. Gombrich, *Sense of Order*, 37–38.

47. Gottfried Semper, *The Four Elements of Architecture and Other Writings*, trans. Harry Francis Mallgrave and Wolfgang Herrmann (Cambridge: Cambridge University Press, 1989), 33.

48. Donald Egbert and Paul Sprague, "In Search of John Edelmann: Architect and Anarchist," *AIA Journal* 45 (February 1966): 35–41.

49. Schafter, *Order of Ornament*, 25–26.

50. Schafter, *Order of Ornament*, 39.

51. Schafter, *Order of Ornament*, 35.

52. Schafter, *Order of Ornament*, 35.

53. Marie Frank, "Emil Lorch: Pure Design and American Architectural Education," *Journal of Architectural Education* (1984–) 57, no. 4 (2004): 28–40.

54. Semper, *Four Elements of Architecture*, 33.

55. Owen Jones, *The Grammar of Ornament* (New York: DK Publishing, Inc., 2001), 472.

56. Schafter, *Order of Ornament*, 23.

57. Semper, *Four Elements of Architecture*, 29.

58. Richard MacCormac, "The Anatomy of Wright's Aesthetic," in *Writings on Wright: Selected Comment on Frank Lloyd Wright*, ed. H. Allen Brooks (Cambridge, Mass.: MIT Press, 1981), 164–73.

59. Rosalind E. Krauss, *The Originality of the Avant-Garde and Other Modernist Myths* (Cambridge, MA: MIT Press, 1986), 158.

60. Gombrich, *Sense of Order*, x.

61. Hubatová-Vacková, *Silent Revolutions*, 25.

62. Eric O'Malley, email message to author, May 28, 2022.

63. Frank Lloyd Wright and Bruce Brooks Pfeiffer, *Frank Lloyd Wright Collected Writings, vol. 1, 1894–1931* (New York; [Scottsdale, AZ]: Rizzoli; Frank Lloyd Wright Foundation, 1992), 21.

64. Wright and Pfeiffer, *Frank Lloyd Wright Collected Writings*, 1:43.

65. Wright and Pfeiffer, *Frank Lloyd Wright Collected Writings*, 1:70.

66. Wright and Pfeiffer, *Frank Lloyd Wright Collected Writings*, 1:81.

67. Wright and Pfeiffer, *Frank Lloyd Wright Collected Writings*, 1:95.

68. Wright and Pfeiffer, *Frank Lloyd Wright Collected Writings*, 1:95.

69. Wright and Pfeiffer, *Frank Lloyd Wright Collected Writings, vol. 2, 1930–1932* (New York; [Scottsdale, AZ]: Rizzoli; Frank Lloyd Wright Foundation, 1992), 55.

70. Wright and Pfeiffer, *Frank Lloyd Wright Collected Writings*, 1:95.

71. Wright and Pfeiffer, *Frank Lloyd Wright Collected Writings*, 1:98.

72. Wright and Pfeiffer, *Frank Lloyd Wright Collected Writings*, 1:105.

73. Wright and Pfeiffer, *Frank Lloyd Wright Collected Writings*, 1:111.

74. Wright and Pfeiffer, *Frank Lloyd Wright Collected Writings*, 1:111.

75. Wright and Pfeiffer, *Frank Lloyd Wright Collected Writings*, 1:180.

76. Wright and Pfeiffer, *Frank Lloyd Wright Collected Writings*, 1:206.

77. Frank Lloyd Wright, "Ethics of Ornament," *Prairie School Review* IV, no. 1 (First Quarter 1967): 16–17.

78. Wright and Pfeiffer, *Frank Lloyd Wright Collected Writings*, 1:295.

79. Wright and Pfeiffer, *Frank Lloyd Wright Collected Writings*, 1:196.

80. Wright and Pfeiffer, *Frank Lloyd Wright Collected Writings*, 1:197.

81. Wright and Pfeiffer, *Frank Lloyd Wright Collected Writings*, 1:320.

82. Wright and Pfeiffer, *Frank Lloyd Wright Collected Writings*, 1:286, 288.

83. Wright and Pfeiffer, *Frank Lloyd Wright Collected Writings*, 1:288.

84. Wright and Pfeiffer, *Frank Lloyd Wright Collected Writings*, 2:21.

85. Wright and Pfeiffer, *Frank Lloyd Wright Collected Writings*, 2:54.

86. Wright and Pfeiffer, *Frank Lloyd Wright Collected Writings*, 2:55.

87. Wright and Pfeiffer, *Frank Lloyd Wright Collected Writings*, 2:55.

88. Wright and Pfeiffer, *Frank Lloyd Wright Collected Writings, vol. 4, 1939–1949* (New York; [Scottsdale, AZ]: Rizzoli; Frank Lloyd Wright Foundation, 1994), 35.

89. Wright and Pfeiffer, *Frank Lloyd Wright Collected Writings, vol. 5, 1949–1959* (New York; [Scottsdale, AZ]: Rizzoli; Frank Lloyd Wright Foundation, 1995), 87.

90. Wright and Pfeiffer, *Frank Lloyd Wright Collected Writings*, 5:92.

91. Wright and Pfeiffer, *Frank Lloyd Wright Collected Writings*, 5:93.

92. Wright and Pfeiffer, *Frank Lloyd Wright Collected Writings*, 5:95.

93. Wright and Pfeiffer, *Frank Lloyd Wright Collected Writings*, 5:96.

94. Wright and Pfeiffer, *Frank Lloyd Wright Collected Writings*, 5:101.

95. Thomas H. Beeby, "The Grammar of Ornament/Ornament as Grammar" in *VIA III Ornament* (Philadelphia: The Graduate School of Fine Arts, University of Pennsylvania, 1977), 11–12.

96. Beeby, "The Grammar of Ornament/Ornament as Grammar," 20.

97. Wright and Pfeiffer, *Frank Lloyd Wright Collected Writings*, 5:80.

98. Wright and Pfeiffer, *Frank Lloyd Wright Collected Writings, vol. 3, 1931–1939* (New York; [Scottsdale, AZ]: Rizzoli; Frank Lloyd Wright Foundation, 1992), 283.

99. Wright, *An Autobiography*, 235.

100. Wright and Pfeiffer, *Frank Lloyd Wright Collected Writings*, 5:101.

101. Wright and Pfeiffer, *Frank Lloyd Wright Collected Writings*, 5:101.

102. Wright and Pfeiffer, *Frank Lloyd Wright Collected Writings*, 5:101.

103. Wright and Pfeiffer, *Frank Lloyd Wright Collected Writings*, 4:273.

104. Wright and Pfeiffer, *Frank Lloyd Wright Collected Writings*, 2:87.

105. George E. Beggs, "The Use of Models in the Solution of Indeterminate Structures," *Franklin Institute Journal* 203, no. 3 (March 1927): 373.

106. Beggs, "Use of Models," 383.

107. Beggs, "Use of Models," 384.

108. Wright and Pfeiffer, *Frank Lloyd Wright Collected Writings*, 5:85.

109. Wright and Pfeiffer, *Frank Lloyd Wright Collected Writings*, 1:237.

110. Wright, *An Autobiography*, 347.

111. Hubatová-Vacková, *Silent Revolutions*, 203.

CHAPTER THREE

112. Frank Lloyd Wright and Bruce Brooks Pfeiffer, *Frank Lloyd Wright Collected Writings, vol. 3, 1931–1939* (New York; [Scottsdale, AZ]: Rizzoli; Frank Lloyd Wright Foundation, 1992), 279.

113. Frank Lloyd Wright and Bruce Brooks Pfeiffer, *Frank Lloyd Wright Collected Writings, vol. 5, 1949–1959* (New York; [Scottsdale, AZ]: Rizzoli; Frank Lloyd Wright Foundation, 1995), 79.

114. Frank Lloyd Wright and Bruce Brooks Pfeiffer, *Frank Lloyd Wright Collected Writings, vol. 1, 1894–1931* (New York; [Scottsdale, AZ]: Rizzoli; Frank Lloyd Wright Foundation, 1992), 296.

115. Wright and Pfeiffer, *Frank Lloyd Wright Collected Writings*, 1:310.

116. R. W. B. Lewis, *The American Adam* (Chicago: University of Chicago Press, 1955), 24.

117. Frank Lloyd Wright and Bruce Brooks Pfeiffer, *Frank Lloyd Wright Collected Writings, vol. 2, 1930–1932* (New York; [Scottsdale, AZ]: Rizzoli; Frank Lloyd Wright Foundation, 1992), 34.

118. Wright and Pfeiffer, *Frank Lloyd Wright Collected Writings*, 1:314.

119. Wright and Pfeiffer, *Frank Lloyd Wright Collected Writings*, 1:86.

120. Wright and Pfeiffer, *Frank Lloyd Wright Collected Writings*, 1:158.

121. Wright and Pfeiffer, *Frank Lloyd Wright Collected Writings*, 1:329.

122. Wright and Pfeiffer, *Frank Lloyd Wright Collected Writings*, 2:31.

123. Wright and Pfeiffer, *Frank Lloyd Wright Collected Writings*, 1:111.

124. Wright and Pfeiffer, *Frank Lloyd Wright Collected Writings*, 1:262.

125. Wright and Pfeiffer, *Frank Lloyd Wright Collected Writings*, 1:59.

126. Wright and Pfeiffer, *Frank Lloyd Wright Collected Writings*, 1:59.

127. Wright and Pfeiffer, *Frank Lloyd Wright Collected Writings*, 1:60.

128. Wright and Pfeiffer, *Frank Lloyd Wright Collected Writings*, 1:60.

129. Wright and Pfeiffer, *Frank Lloyd Wright Collected Writings*, 1:231.

130. Wright and Pfeiffer, *Frank Lloyd Wright Collected Writings*, 1:195.

131. Wright and Pfeiffer, *Frank Lloyd Wright Collected Writings*, 1:59.

132. Wright and Pfeiffer, *Frank Lloyd Wright Collected Writings*, 1:61.

133. Wright and Pfeiffer, *Frank Lloyd Wright Collected Writings*, 1:68.

134. Wright and Pfeiffer, *Frank Lloyd Wright Collected Writings*, 1:61.

135. Wright and Pfeiffer, *Frank Lloyd Wright Collected Writings*, 1:64.

136. Wright and Pfeiffer, *Frank Lloyd Wright Collected Writings*, 1:66.

137. Wright and Pfeiffer, *Frank Lloyd Wright Collected Writings*, 1:194.

138. Wright and Pfeiffer, *Frank Lloyd Wright Collected Writings*, 1:210.

139. Wright and Pfeiffer, *Frank Lloyd Wright Collected Writings*, 1:210.

140. Wright and Pfeiffer, *Frank Lloyd Wright Collected Writings*, 1:241.

141. Wright and Pfeiffer, *Frank Lloyd Wright Collected Writings*, 1:214.

142. Wright and Pfeiffer, *Frank Lloyd Wright Collected Writings*, 1:262.

143. Wright and Pfeiffer, *Frank Lloyd Wright Collected Writings*, 2:68.

144. Wright and Pfeiffer, *Frank Lloyd Wright Collected Writings*, 1:230.

145. Wright and Pfeiffer, *Frank Lloyd Wright Collected Writings*, 1:210.

146. Wright and Pfeiffer, *Frank Lloyd Wright Collected Writings*, 1:231.

147. Wright and Pfeiffer, *Frank Lloyd Wright Collected Writings*, 1:231.

148. Wright and Pfeiffer, *Frank Lloyd Wright Collected Writings*, 2:88.

149. Wright and Pfeiffer, *Frank Lloyd Wright Collected Writings*, 1:231.

150. Wright and Pfeiffer, *Frank Lloyd Wright Collected Writings*, 1:243.

151. Wright and Pfeiffer, *Frank Lloyd Wright Collected Writings*, 1:263.

152. Wright and Pfeiffer, *Frank Lloyd Wright Collected Writings*, 1:250.

153. Wright and Pfeiffer, *Frank Lloyd Wright Collected Writings*, 1:164.

154. Wright and Pfeiffer, *Frank Lloyd Wright Collected Writings*, 1:184.

155. Wright and Pfeiffer, *Frank Lloyd Wright Collected Writings*, 1:125.

156. Wright and Pfeiffer, *Frank Lloyd Wright Collected Writings*, 1:125.

157. Wright and Pfeiffer, *Frank Lloyd Wright Collected Writings*, 1:119.

158. Wright and Pfeiffer, *Frank Lloyd Wright Collected Writings*, 1:124.

159. Wright and Pfeiffer, *Frank Lloyd Wright Collected Writings*, 1:247.

160. Wright and Pfeiffer, *Frank Lloyd Wright Collected Writings*, 1:124.

161. Wright and Pfeiffer, *Frank Lloyd Wright Collected Writings*, 1:292.

162. Wright and Pfeiffer, *Frank Lloyd Wright Collected Writings*, 1:120.

163. Wright and Pfeiffer, *Frank Lloyd Wright Collected Writings*, 1:23.

164. Wright and Pfeiffer, *Frank Lloyd Wright Collected Writings*, 1:22.

165. Wright and Pfeiffer, *Frank Lloyd Wright Collected Writings*, 1:118.

166. Wright and Pfeiffer, *Frank Lloyd Wright Collected Writings*, 1:119.

167. Wright and Pfeiffer, *Frank Lloyd Wright Collected Writings*, 1:247, 248.

168. Wright and Pfeiffer, *Frank Lloyd Wright Collected Writings*, 1:123.

169. Wright and Pfeiffer, *Frank Lloyd Wright Collected Writings*, 2:32.

170. Wright and Pfeiffer, *Frank Lloyd Wright Collected Writings*, 1:119.

171. Wright and Pfeiffer, *Frank Lloyd Wright Collected Writings*, 1:259, 260.

172. Wright and Pfeiffer, *Frank Lloyd Wright Collected Writings*, 1:117.

173. Wright and Pfeiffer, *Frank Lloyd Wright Collected Writings*, 1:125.

174. Wright and Pfeiffer, *Frank Lloyd Wright Collected Writings*, 1:247.

175. Achim Borchardt-Hume, Gloria Groom, Caitlin Haskell, and Natalia Sedlina, eds., *Cezanne*, (Chicago: Art Institute of Chicago, 2022), 57, 59n44.

176. Wright and Pfeiffer, *Frank Lloyd Wright Collected Writings*, 1:20–26.

177. Wright and Pfeiffer, *Frank Lloyd Wright Collected Writings*, 1:31, 32.

178. Wright and Pfeiffer, *Frank Lloyd Wright Collected Writings*, 1:89.

179. Wright and Pfeiffer, *Frank Lloyd Wright Collected Writings*, 1:263.

180. Wright and Pfeiffer, *Frank Lloyd Wright Collected Writings*, 2:58.

181. Wright and Pfeiffer, *Frank Lloyd Wright Collected Writings*, 1:263.

182. Wright and Pfeiffer, *Frank Lloyd Wright Collected Writings*, 1:100.

183. Wright and Pfeiffer, *Frank Lloyd Wright Collected Writings*, 1:127.

184. Wright and Pfeiffer, *Frank Lloyd Wright Collected Writings*, 1:190.

185. Wright and Pfeiffer, *Frank Lloyd Wright Collected Writings*, 2:32.

186. Frank Lloyd Wright and Bruce Brooks Pfeiffer, *Frank Lloyd Wright Collected Writings, vol. 4, 1939–1949* (New York; [Scottsdale, AZ]: Rizzoli; Frank Lloyd Wright Foundation, 1994), 53, 287; Wright and Pfeiffer, *Frank Lloyd Wright Collected Writings*, 1:105.

187. Wright and Pfeiffer, *Frank Lloyd Wright Collected Writings*, 1:288.

188. Wright and Pfeiffer, *Frank Lloyd Wright Collected Writings*, 1:120.

189. Wright and Pfeiffer, *Frank Lloyd Wright Collected Writings*, 1:259, 260, 247.

190. Wright and Pfeiffer, *Frank Lloyd Wright Collected Writings*, 1:146.

191. Wright and Pfeiffer, *Frank Lloyd Wright Collected Writings*, 2:100.

192. Wright and Pfeiffer, *Frank Lloyd Wright Collected Writings*, 2:32.

193. Wright and Pfeiffer, *Frank Lloyd Wright Collected Writings*, 1:106.

194. Wright and Pfeiffer, *Frank Lloyd Wright Collected Writings*, 1:98.

195. Wright and Pfeiffer, *Frank Lloyd Wright Collected Writings*, 1:137.

196. Wright and Pfeiffer, *Frank Lloyd Wright Collected Writings*, 1:129.

197. Wright and Pfeiffer, *Frank Lloyd Wright Collected Writings*, 1:200.

198. Henry-Russell Hitchcock, "Frank Lloyd Wright and the 'Academic Tradition' of the Early Eighteen-Nineties," *Journal of the Warburg and Courtauld Institutes* 7 (1944): 46–63.

199. Hitchcock, "Frank Lloyd Wright and the 'Academic Tradition' of the Early Eighteen-Nineties," 63.

200. Wright and Pfeiffer, *Frank Lloyd Wright Collected Writings*, 1:122.

201. Wright and Pfeiffer, *Frank Lloyd Wright Collected Writings*, 1:256.

202. Wright and Pfeiffer, *Frank Lloyd Wright Collected Writings*, 1:256.

203. Wright and Pfeiffer, *Frank Lloyd Wright Collected Writings*, 1:213.

204. Wright and Pfeiffer, *Frank Lloyd Wright Collected Writings*, 1:136.

205. Wright and Pfeiffer, *Frank Lloyd Wright Collected Writings*, 1:107.

206. Wright and Pfeiffer, *Frank Lloyd Wright Collected Writings*, 1:44.

207. Wright and Pfeiffer, *Frank Lloyd Wright Collected Writings*, 1:166.

208. Wright and Pfeiffer, *Frank Lloyd Wright Collected Writings*, 1:90.

209. Wright and Pfeiffer, *Frank Lloyd Wright Collected Writings*, 2:59.

CHAPTER FOUR

210. Le Corbusier, Oscar Stonorov, Willy Boesiger, and Pierre Jeanneret. *Le Corbusier et Pierre Jeanneret: Oeuvre complète de 1910–1929; nouv. éd.* (Zürich: H. Girsberger, 1937), 33.

211. Vincent Scully. *Modern Architecture.* (New York: Braziller, 1984), 31.

212. Frank Lloyd Wright and Bruce Brooks Pfeiffer, *Frank Lloyd Wright Collected Writings, vol. 2, 1930–1932* (New York: [Scottsdale, AZ], Rizzoli; Frank Lloyd Wright Foundation, 1992), 56.

213. Frank Lloyd Wright and Bruce Brooks Pfeiffer, *Frank Lloyd Wright Collected Writings, vol. 1, 1894–1931* (New York: [Scottsdale, AZ], Rizzoli; Frank Lloyd Wright Foundation, 1992), 212.

214. Louis H. Sullivan, *Kindergarten Chats, and Other Writings* (New York: Dover Publications, 1979), 227.

215. Sullivan, *Kindergarten Chats*, 124.

216. Wright and Pfeiffer, *Frank Lloyd Wright Collected Writings*, 2:87.

217. Sidney K. Robinson, "The Romantic Classicism of the Prairie School," *Inland Architect* 35, no. 3 (May/June 1991): 42–45.

218. Richard MacCormac, "The Anatomy of Wright's Aesthetic," in *Writings on Wright: Selected Comment on Frank Lloyd Wright*, ed. H. Allen Brooks (Cambridge, MA: MIT Press, 1981), 164–73.

219. Wright and Pfeiffer, *Frank Lloyd Wright Collected Writings*, 2:51.

220. Video interview with William Wesley Peters, November 28, 1989. Filmed in Wes's apartment, Taliesin West.

221. Frank Lloyd Wright, Yukio Futagawa, and Bruce Brooks Pfeiffer, *Frank Lloyd Wright, selected houses. 6, 6* (Tokyo: A.D.A. Edita, 1991), 98.

222. *Pope-Leighey House*, National Trust for Historic Preservation, Washington, D.C., 2006, 70.

CONCLUSION

223. Wright and Pfeiffer, *Frank Lloyd Wright Collected Writings*, 1:242.

INDEX

Adler and Sullivan, 61,191

An Autobiography; Frank Lloyd Wright, 1, 2, 15, 82, 87

Architectural Record 49, 69, 93, 103

"Art and Craft of the Machine"; Frank Lloyd Wright, 10, 14, 49, 69, 77, 98, 186

Auditorium Building, Banqueting Hall, 20–39, 43, 44, 73, 111,

Auerbach, Erich; *Mimesis*, 46

Bach House, 146, 147

Beeby, Thomas, 81

Beethoven Fifth Symphony, 10

Beggs, George E., 84, 85, 171

Boynton House, 153, 154, 155

Cezanne, 117

Chermayeff, Serge, 138

Cole, Henry, 64

Cuvier, Georges, 61, 62

Dow, Arthur, 62

Dyce, William, 59, 60

Edelmann, John, 61, 74

Eliot, T. S; *The Waste Land*, 46

Evans House, 143, 144, 145

Fallingwater, xiii, xiv, 78, 159, 160, 178, 182, 187

Froebel, Friedrich 12

Genius and the Mobocracy; Frank Lloyd Wright 8, 10, 67, 73, 79

Gombrich, Ernst; *A Sense of Order*, 66

Gothic, 23, 38, 56, 57, 71, 80, 83, 121, 142, 169

Guggenheim Museum, 169

Hardy House, 5, 6, 108,

Hillside Assembly, 157, 158, 159, 162

Hitchcock, Henry Russell, 58, 126

Holloway, John, 46, 47, 48

Hubatova-Vackova, Lada, 66

Hugo, Victor, 57, 95

Imperial Hotel, 5, 15, 49, 50, 72, 105

Jacobs House, 176

Japan, 50, 71, 107, 118, 126, 127

Japanese Prints, 33, 71, 107, 108, 110, 111, 112, 113, 114,122

Jewish Museum, New York, 48

Johnson, Philip, 48, 58

Jones, Owen, 63

Kahn Lectures, Princeton Lectures; Frank Lloyd Wright 10, 14, 70, 75, 80, 84, 85, 96, 97

L'Eplattenier, Charles, 133

Le Corbusier, 15, 133–34

Loos, Adolf, 58

MacCormac, Richard; tartan grid, 65, 66, 84, 161

Mahony, Marion, 108, 168, 204

Mendelsohn, Eric, 186

Meyer May House, 162, 163

Midway Gardens, 5, 19, 20, 59, 76, 170, 171

Morris, William, 98

Museum of Modern Art, 5, 59, 87

Northrup, F.S.C., 109, 110

O'Malley, Eric, 67

Oak Park Playhouse, 19, 20, 21

Ocatillo, 81, 172, 173

Palladio, 80, 95

Perrine, Laurence, 4

Peters, William Wesley, 175

Pew House, 174, 175

Pfeiffer, Bruce Brooks, 96

Phoenix Art Museum, 15, 72

Plato, 114, 115, 116

Pope-Leighey House, 175, 180, 181, 182, 183

Pragnell, Peter, 133

Robie House, 153, 155, 156, 161

Ross, Denman W., 62

Ruprich-Robert, Victor, 43

Ruskin, John, 56, 57, 58, 60, 80, 98

Russell, Edward Stuart, 62

Saint-Hilaire, Geoffroy, 62

Samuelson, Tim, 22

Sandburg, Carl, 92

Schafter, Debra, 59

Scully, Vincent, 134

Semper, Gottfried, 61, 63, 64, 83

Stewart House, 148, 149,150

Stockman House, 143, 144, 145

Sullivan, Louis, 1, 7, 8, 9, 10, 16, 17, 19-23, 30, 33-46, 49, 51-53, 59, 61, 67, 69, 73, 74, 76, 79, 80, 81, 85, 86, 88, 93, 100, 101, 111, 112, 122, 125, 126, 135, 136, 140, 142, 185, 186, 188

Taliesin, Wisconsin, 51, 52, 104, 110, 119, 166, 172, 177, 181, 183, 186, 187

Taliesin West, 133, 134, 136, 172, 177

Textile Block Houses, 78, 82, 105, 177, 178

Thomas House, 162

"Two Lectures on Architecture"; Frank Lloyd Wright, 10

Unity Temple, 10, 11, 12, 13, 49, 51, 52, 55, 81, 87, 119, 168, 169, 183, 188

Van de Velde, Henri 87

van de Ven, Cornelius, 49

Viollet-le-Duc, 57

Warn, Bob, 110

Wasmuth, 71, 75, 108, 112

Wendingen, 49

Willey House, 162, 163,164, 165, 166, 167, 168

Wornum, Ralph, 60